Intercontinental Terminals Company LLC

December 2013

Dear ITC Friend,

We at Intercontinental Terminals Company LLC want to thank you for your valued business relationship during 2013. We look forward to 2014 and our continued partnership. On behalf of everyone at ITC we wish you and your family a Merry Christmas and a safe and prosperous New Year.

Yours very truly,

Bernt A. Netland
President & CEO

Richard C. Merz
Senior Vice President,
Sales and Marketing

Steve Turchi
Sr. Vice-President,
Business Development

Harold Thomas
Sales Manager

John C. Everett
Customer Service Manager

ITC is a safe and dedicated partner whose associates are recognized as proud leaders in customer care and operational excellence.

TEXAS
THEN & NOW

WILLIAM DYLAN POWELL

PHOTOGRAPHED BY
KEN FITZGERALD

THUNDER BAY
P·R·E·S·S

San Diego, California

TEXAS

THEN & NOW INTRODUCTION

You might have met them. You might have them in the family. Heck, you might even be one of them. I'm talking about people who are fanatical about Texas. People who identify as Texans first, and everything else later. People who fly the Texas flag at their homes, on their car or truck—and maybe even have it tattooed somewhere.

There are millions of such people in Texas, from a wide variety of backgrounds. And whether you find such folk endearing, annoying, or somewhere in between, you've got to ask yourself: What kind of place produces such die-hard loyalty? This book is a visual exploration of how Texas has, and has not, changed over the years. And as you'll see, change has been plentiful. A Texan from the days of the republic wouldn't recognize much in the concrete and glass landscape of Houston, the sprawling suburbs of Dallas–Fort Worth, or the high-tech research campuses around Austin. The baseball hat has replaced the cowboy hat in much of Texas, and a smartphone is more ubiquitous than a pair of cowboy boots.

Three major trends have reshaped the landscape from the Red River to the Rio Grande: rapid urbanization and population increase; shifting demographics and cultural diversity; and amazing levels of economic prosperity.

These days, more Texans live in ranch-style homes rather than actual ranches. Since before the days of the Republic of Texas (1836–45), when

TEXAS
THEN & NOW

Thunder Bay Press
An imprint of the Baker & Taylor Publishing Group
10350 Barnes Canyon Road, San Diego, CA 92121
www.thunderbaybooks.com

Produced by Salamander Books,
an imprint of Anova Books Ltd.
10 Southcombe Street, London W14 0RA, UK

"Then and Now" is a registered trademark of Anova Books Ltd.

Library of Congress Cataloging-in-Publication Data

Powell, William Dylan.
  Texas then & now / William Dylan Powell.
     pages cm. -- (Then & now)
  ISBN-13: 978-1-60710-890-0 (hardback)
  ISBN-10: 1-60710-890-9
1. Texas--Pictorial works. 2. Texas--History, Local--Pictorial works. 3. Texas--
Buildings, structures, etc.--Pictorial works. 4. Historic buildings--Texas--Pictorial
works. 5. Repeat photography--Texas. I. Title. II. Title: Texas then and now.
  F387.P68 2013
  976.4--dc23
                          2013020549

Printed in China

1 2 3 4 5 17 16 15 14 13

PICTURE CREDITS

The publisher wishes to thank the following for kindly supplying the photographs
that appear in this book:

"Then" photographs:

Austin History Center, page 18.
Corbis, pages 26, 102 (bottom), 128, 130, 131, 136, and 140.
Corpus Christi Public Library, pages 44, 46, and 52.
Dallas Public Library, pages 108, 112, 114, 116, 118, 120, and 122.
Getty Images, pages 42, 48, 49, 70, 76, and 126.
Houston Public Library, pages 58, 62, 66, 68, 71, 72, and 74.
Library of Congress, page 8 (bottom), 17 (top), 24, 28, 34, 35, 40, 42, 43, 50, 54, 56,
57, 60, 64, 73, 78, 80, 82, 84, 85, 86, 88, 90, 92, 93, 94, 95, 96, 100, 102, 104, 106, 107,
124, 126 (bottom), 132, 134, 138, 142, and 143.
The Portal to Texas History (http://texashistory.unt.edu), pages 8, 10, 12, 14, 15, 16,
17 (bottom), 20, 21, 22, 110, 111, and 123.
Texas A&M University, pages 98 and 99.
University of Texas, San Antonio, pages 30, 32, 36, and 38.

"Now" photographs:

All "Now" images were taken by Ken Fitzgerald (© Anova Image Library) except
for the following: Getty Images, page 77; Robert Heine (www.heinefilm.com),
pages 128–143, El Paso and Amarillo.

Anova Books is committed to respecting the intellectual property rights of others.
We have therefore taken all reasonable efforts to ensure that the reproduction of all
content on these pages is done with the full consent of copyright owners. If you are
aware of any unintentional omissions, please contact the company directly so that
any necessary corrections may be made for future editions.

Texas was its own country, the region was largely agrarian, with cattle ranchers, massive cotton plantations, and small-time subsistence farmers in abundance. In fact, right up until the beginning of the twentieth century, it looked as if the Texas landscape would share the same rural economic future as Kansas or Mississippi.

But the gusher at Spindletop in January 1901—and the subsequent oil boom—changed everything. Oil brought instant wealth and industry to the area, first to southeast Texas and eventually almost statewide. All that capital brought more jobs—and the communities, people, and infrastructure to support them. Today, Texas is a little over 82 percent urban. More than 17 million Texans live in the city, while 3.6 million live in rural areas. Since 2000, Texas's population has grown at a rate twice that of the rest of the nation. Traditional Texas-style ranch culture still abounds, however. The top-selling vehicle in the state is the Ford F-150 pickup truck, despite the fact that most are used for making trips to the grocery store or commuting to an office.

The face of Texas is also changing. Though the initial demographics of Texas's founding pioneers were more diverse than most people realized, the state is now more heterogeneous than ever. Dozens of cultures helped make Texas what it is today. From the Spanish and Mexican settlers in pre-republic years to the German and Irish immigrants in the nineteenth century to the contemporary Asian population, each added something. At the same time, the state has not strayed far from its roots as a colony of the Mexican republic. In 1980 the Hispanic population was around 3 million. The state projects that by 2040, there will be 18.8 million Hispanic Texans—all seeking the prosperity for which Texas has become legend.

People have always come to Texas to get ahead. Early Anglo-American settlers in the 1800s would abandon their homes and write "GTT"—Gone to Texas—on their front doors. Once here, they received land in exchange for industry. History is repeating itself today, with continued migration to Texas from other states, lured by, among other things, no state income taxes. Over a hundred Fortune 500 companies call Texas home. It's the biggest exporter of any state. It's a world energy leader, and the only state with its own independent electrical grid. And in a time when many Americans are struggling, Texas created 279,000 jobs in 2012.

In a recent ranking by *Forbes* magazine of the best cities for jobs in the United States, the top four were Houston, Dallas, Austin, and Fort Worth (San Antonio came in at number six). If Texas were a nation, its economy would be the fourteenth largest in the world. Today's white-hot economic prosperity would surely make Texas's founding fathers—who risked not only their wealth but their very lives for independence—proud.

But while so much has changed since Texas's early days, one thing hasn't. It's something visible in all of these photographs—and, at the same time, in none of them. It's the mind-set of those who call Texas home, whether by birth or by choice. It may sound hokey if you've not experienced it yourself, but the spirit of what it means to be a Texan is the same for today's Austin accountant as it was for yesterday's Fort Worth farmer. It's a spirit of determination, a spirit of optimism, a drive to find a way to get things done regardless of obstacles and naysayers. It means talking only when you've got something to say—and then keeping your word after the fact.

You'll see that spirit in the people and places showcased on these pages, from El Paso to Beaumont, from southern Texas to downtown Dallas. You'll see it reflected in the structures Texans have created then and now. You'll see it here in this book just like you see it in the faces of the cowboys mending fences on the western plains or the bankers on the trading floors in Houston. And, just maybe, in the mirror.

The buildings may come and go. The fortunes may ebb and flow. The names on the signs may change over the decades. But no matter what the future has in store for the people and places of Texas, we'll always be able to build on the Texan spirit—and we'll always be grateful to Texans of the past for keeping that legacy alive.

Congress Avenue, Austin, 1913   *p. 14*

The Alamo, San Antonio, c. 1920   *p. 26*

Stinson Field, San Antonio, 1917   *p. 36*

Menger Hotel, San Antonio, c. 1930   *p. 40*

Rodd Field, Corpus Christi, 1942   *p. 42*

North Beach, Corpus Christi, 1939   *p. 54*

Old Cotton Exchange, Houston, c. 1905   *p. 62*

Rice University, Houston, c. 1920   *p. 68*

Houston Astrodome, 1965   *p. 72*

USS Texas, Houston, 1920   p. 78

Galveston Historic District, c. 1965   p. 90

Spindletop, Beaumont, 1901   p. 94

Texas A&M, College Station, c. 1930   p. 98

Suspension Bridge, Waco, c. 1940   p. 102

Old Red Courthouse, Dallas, c. 1925   p. 108

Cotton Bowl, Dallas, 1951   p. 120

Fort Worth Stockyards, c. 1940   p. 126

Mexican Adobe House, El Paso, 1907   p. 134

c.1915

CONGRESS AVENUE BRIDGE, AUSTIN
A grand gateway to the city of Austin

ABOVE: The Congress Avenue Bridge sometime in the 1910s. It is one of several bridges that have crossed the Colorado River in this spot (the first was a pontoon bridge, put into service around 1869). The Congress Avenue Bridge was opened in April 1910 at a cost of over $200,000—a substantial sum at the time. Just over 945 feet long and 60 feet wide, the concrete arch bridge was built by the King Bridge Company of Ohio and was designed to hold 2,000 pounds of weight per square foot. Its width, protected sidewalks, and decorative concrete railing made it popular with the public right away. Streetcar lines were incorporated into the road surface, unlike on other bridges, which had to be substantially altered to accommodate streetcar lines. The telltale dark splotches on the white concrete—indicating the presence of equestrian traffic—show that a built-in, horse-free sidewalk was a fine idea.

c.1940

ABOVE: Today, the bridge is formally known as the Ann W. Richards Congress Avenue Bridge, named after the outspoken forty-fifth governor of Texas. The bridge stayed true to its original design over the years. As streetcars fell out of favor and automobiles and city buses took hold, the rail lines were removed to make room for more vehicles in the 1950s. From the late 1970s to 1980, the bridge underwent a massive overhaul. Not long after, around 1.5 million Mexican freetail bats came to roost under the bridge, nestling within gaps in the bridge's bottom flanges one summer in the early 1980s. Since then, the bats have returned each summer to reside under the bridge. Now many call it "the bat bridge," and stop in on summer evenings to see the world's largest urban bat colony. In fact, in the summer months there are more bats than people in Austin. The tall building on the left is the Austonian—the tallest residential building west of the Mississippi River.

LEFT: Fast forward to around 1940 and the streetcar lines are gone, but Checker Lumber has survived the Depression, and the view is very much the same.

1946

PARAMOUNT THEATRE, AUSTIN

Local businessmen rescued it from the wrecking ball in the 1970s

ABOVE: When the Paramount Theatre at 713 Congress Avenue presented its first show in 1915, it was known as the Majestic Theatre. The building was designed by architect John Eberson of Chicago, who designed over a thousand theaters. It was initially a stage for vaudeville performances, and Harry Houdini once appeared on the bill, showcasing his famous escapology act. The theater adapted to a changing market as silent films took the place of vaudeville, and were later replaced by talking pictures. In 1930 its owners embarked on a major overhaul—including new upholstered seats, a state-of-the-art sound system, carpeting, and a new name: the Paramount Theatre. It was still used for live performances, but by the 1950s it was almost exclusively a movie venue. This photo was taken just after World War II. The theater made a sizable contribution to the war effort, selling $8.4 million in war bonds.

ABOVE: In 1973 the old movie house was scheduled for demolition, but three local businessmen came to the rescue by starting a nonprofit organization and restoring the theater. By 1975 it was back in business, showing classic flicks like *Citizen Kane* for just fifty cents. In 1977 the building was listed on the National Register of Historic Places. Throughout the 1970s, the theater saw both renovations and struggles. But by the 1980s, national touring companies were hitting the live stage. Comedians such as Rodney Dangerfield and George Carlin played the Paramount. It even hosted a few exclusive Hollywood premieres (such as *The Best Little Whorehouse in Texas*, with Burt Reynolds, Dolly Parton, and Jim Nabors in attendance). Now it is not only thriving but has annexed the State Theatre next door; together they host a range of film, dance, and stage performances.

c.1910

OLD TRAVIS COUNTY COURTHOUSE

One of many Austin buildings designed by architect Jacob L. Larmour

LEFT: Several buildings served as the Travis County Courthouse over the years, including, at first, a log cabin. But none have been as distinctive as the one built in 1875, shown here in the early 1900s. This was the first truly elegant courthouse in the county; its predecessor was a simple, two-story concrete affair. Standing at the southwest corner of Eleventh Street and Congress Avenue, right across from the capitol building, its inspiring French Second Empire architectural style was very much in vogue at the time. The three-story building was made of local limestone, and sported mansard roofs, intricate ironwork cresting, and huge decorative dormers. The building's architect was Jacob L. Larmour, who was appointed as the official state architect of Texas the year the courthouse was built. Larmour designed several buildings on Congress Avenue, including the First National Bank (1873), the Travis County Jail and Jailer's House (1875), and some commercial buildings.

1932

ABOVE: Like many of its kind, the old building was both a courthouse and jail. Writer William Sydney Porter (better known as O. Henry) was held there while facing charges of embezzlement of the First Austin National Bank, for which he had worked as a teller in 1894 before his writing career took off. By 1927 the courthouse was still grand, but many considered it to be too old-fashioned. By 1930 the county had chosen a new site for its courthouse on Tenth and Guadalupe Streets on the north end of Wooldridge Park. In 1931 a new Art Deco–style courthouse (left) was completed, and the old 1875 building was remodeled to some extent. It was rechristened the Walton Building and assigned for use by various state agencies; it was demolished in 1964. Today, the only evidence of its existence is a historical marker in a parking lot.

1913

CONGRESS AVENUE, AUSTIN
The emblematic street at the heart of the city

c.1947

LEFT: Congress Avenue has always been the city's most prominent roadway—Austin was designed to that effect by its first mayor, Edwin Waller. Some of Austin's first small shops, saloons, and ragtag government buildings were built along the avenue, and were eventually replaced by grander and bigger structures as the city grew. By the 1940s, the city had the feel of a bustling metropolis (above). Looking up Congress Avenue, the capitol building still loomed large over the landscape, but everything else was in bloom. The Norwood Tower on the far left had sprung up in 1929, and at the time it was the tallest building in Austin after the capitol. It was also the first office building to be air-conditioned. The distinctive curved design of the Littlefield Building (1910) frames the right side of both archival photos, with passersby rushing past the city's most prestigious financial building of its day. In the distance on the right can be seen the Paramount Theatre.

ABOVE: In the thick of it all, this is still the street most people envision when they think of Austin (and not just because it's home to the Continental Club). The Norwood Tower, the Littlefield Building (second on the right with the flag at half-mast), and many other original buildings are still on the scene. So many historic structures remain on Congress Avenue that the roadway itself from First Street to the capitol building was listed in the National Register of Historic Places in 1979. The city has grown a lot taller, as have the trees. Locals call the avenue south of Lady Bird Lake South Congress, or "SoCo" for short— a trendy haunt for copious hipsters on Congress Avenue from around Johanna Street to Gibson Street. Downtown, Congress Avenue remains a pedestrian-friendly spot that still has the same kinetic energy as it did when streetcars and horses and buggies clopped along the road.

1889

STATE CAPITOL, AUSTIN
Today, the building is as vast underground as it is aboveground

ABOVE: Today's Texas State Capitol Building is actually the fourth state capitol to hold court in Austin. Its Renaissance Revival design was determined by a national contest, won by Detroit architect Elijah E. Myers. To finance the construction of the capitol, Texas legislators took a pass on the typical bonds or federal reserve currency most states used in favor of good, old-fashioned Texas land. In what was one of the biggest barter transactions in the history of the region, the State of Texas paid a contractor for the construction of its current capitol with three million acres of land in the panhandle. Built of red granite with a Goddess of Liberty statue atop its dome, the building was paid for in property holdings that were then valued at around $1.5 million.

ABOVE: A view of West Austin, taken from the dome of the capitol between 1887 and 1894.

BELOW: The senate chamber of the capitol around 1910.

c.1890

c.1910

ABOVE: The capitol is more vibrant and verdant than ever. A fire in the 1980s significantly damaged the east end of the building—and gave the state an excuse to remodel and make upgrades. In 1985 the original zinc Goddess of Liberty statue was removed via helicopter and replaced with an aluminum replica in 1986. The original statue can still be seen on the capitol grounds. The lavish Governor's Public Reception Room, designed for hosting VIPs, received an upgrade in 1987, and a $75 million underground extension was built in the early 1990s, making the building as big underground as it is aboveground in terms of square footage. In 1997 the park surrounding the capitol got an $8 million renovation. Fittingly, it is the biggest state capitol building in the United States. A hundred years after the building's dedication, the land that was bartered for its construction was valued at approximately $7 billion.

1936

UNIVERSITY OF TEXAS TOWER
Designed to be the "biggest bookshelf" in Texas

ABOVE: The Main Building at the University of Texas (shown here still under construction), with its distinctive 307-foot-tall tower, was completed in 1937. Designed by Paul Cret of Philadelphia, it immediately became a symbol of Longhorn pride. This is not the original Main Building, however. The first Main Building was built in 1882, standing where the current tower now stands. It was razed in 1934. Originally, the new tower was to be the state's "biggest bookshelf"—students on the second floor would request a book, and librarians on the upper floors would send books down using an eighteen-story dumbwaiter. The tower was topped with a fifty-six-bell carillon. The tower's construction came on the heels of the Great Depression, which actually caused university leaders to accelerate construction (and provide more jobs). Through political connections, the university secured $1.8 million in Works Progress Administration funds to finish the building. The building was dubbed the "UT Skyscraper" because it towered over Austin's skyline.

ABOVE: Today, the UT Tower doesn't seem like much of a skyscraper—but it's still large in terms of cultural iconography. The library-via-dumbwaiter scheme proved too much work, and today the Main Building is mostly administrative in nature, although it still houses the Miriam Lutcher Stark Library. Many professors have offices in the building, and one can only speculate about how status is correlated to office floors. These days, the tower is lit at night in white, the colors changing on special occasions (including a somber gray during times of mourning). During commencement ceremonies, the lights spell out the year of the graduating class. Some of the old library's features, such as its two spacious reading rooms, still remain. The view from the observation deck is as breathtaking as ever. Over the years, the University of Texas has become a symbol of academic achievement, prosperity, and liberal thinking worldwide—and the tower has come to symbolize the school, its accomplishments, and its ambitions.

DRISKILL HOTEL, AUSTIN
Defying the economic odds to stay in business

1888

LEFT: In 1888 the Driskill was considered one of the most exquisite hotels in Texas. The hotel's namesake was Jesse Lincoln Driskill—a cattleman of Irish descent who made a fortune in the mid-1800s (and then lost it, and then made another). Driskill bought this entire city block for $7,500 in 1885. The hotel opened in 1886. It was designed by Jasper N. Preston, who was inspired by Boston's Ames Building. It originally sported sixty steam-heated rooms and four suites on the second floor. But it was more than just a hotel. It was the center of Austin social life, where the great and the good met to sip champagne at extravagant balls, and state politicians sealed deals over a handshake. Historians say its dining room was the fanciest restaurant in town for years after the hotel opened, and gentlemen could stop in for dinner, a drink at the bar, a game of billiards, or a haircut.

BELOW: As opulent as the Driskill was, its fortunes were every bit as volatile as that of its namesake. Just a few months after opening, the place was in the red and the turnover among hotel ownership resembled that of its waiting staff. But every new owner kept the lights on, and it never lost its magic. In 1923 one savvy owner subdivided the rooms to double its occupancy (and revenue potential). In 1930 a fifteen-story annex was added, along with adornments such as eight mirrors once owned by the empress of Mexico, back when there was such a thing. Every time financial ruin seemed imminent, somebody saved it. Today, Austin without the Driskill is almost unthinkable. It's still where those in the know stay when visiting the Texas capital. And it's not only every bit as grand as it was in the 1880s; it now offers an energy, gravitas, and provenance that no franchise hotel will ever replicate.

ABOVE: The Driskill Hotel looms large beyond the intersection of Sixth Street and Congress Avenue in this photo looking to the east.

SIXTH STREET, AUSTIN

Once known as Pecan Street, this historic district is the center of Austin's vibrant music scene

ABOVE: This shot shows the south side of East Sixth Street at Neches in 1968. At the time, Austin's two biggest moneymakers—education and government—were booming. This street was once known as Pecan Street rather than Sixth. In Austin's old days, all east–west streets were named after Texas trees and all north–south streets were named after Texas rivers; Pecan Street was renamed Sixth Street in 1884. The original businesses in these commercial Victorian buildings thrived because this was one of the best roads coming into town from the east, as it was not too hilly or prone to flooding—which is important when driving a mule train through the mud. The late 1960s were arguably Sixth Street's lowest years, when downtown wasn't very popular and many older buildings in the area were either abandoned or in a shameful state of repair. At the time, most Austin residents had scant reason to visit Sixth Street in their daily lives.

c.1925

ABOVE: Sixth Street has grown with the city. By the 1970s, it was ground zero for Austin's live music scene. It was an accepting place, where budding musicians could get a foothold—and audiences could hear something new. As Austin musician Paul Ray once described it: "There were rednecks and long-hairs sitting next to one another at the bar telling jokes to one another. People got along. It was just a different scene." Sixth Street venues like Antone's, originally at Sixth and Brazos, helped transform the area—hosting Stevie Ray Vaughn, Bob Dylan, B. B. King, Sam and Dave, the Fabulous Thunderbirds, John Lee Hooker, and more. Antone's has moved several times and isn't on Sixth Street any longer, but Sixth Street today is a world-famous entertainment district known for live music venues stretching from around Congress Avenue to Interstate 35. In 1975 an entire nine-block area labeled the Sixth Street Historic District was listed on the National Register of Historic Places.

LEFT: Looking west down Sixth Street around 1925, from the top of the Scarborough Building at Sixth and Congress.

c.1900

MOONLIGHT TOWERS, AUSTIN

Towering over the city for more than a century

ABOVE: In the late 1800s, many American and European cities found that the running and maintenance of numerous small streetlights could get expensive, so huge lights designed to brighten several blocks were built. Most were carbon-arc lamps that gave off a harsh light. In 1894 the Austin City Council approved the installation of "moonlight towers" citywide. Rather than build anew, Austin purchased thirty-one towers from the City of Detroit—which had to sell them because of union intervention in their operation. The moonlight towers were installed on the streets in 1895 at a height of 165 feet. Each radiated a 3,000-foot circle of light, and most of the citizens thought they were a wonderful convenience. The lights were converted to incandescent lamps in the 1920s, and then to mercury vapor in the 1930s.

24

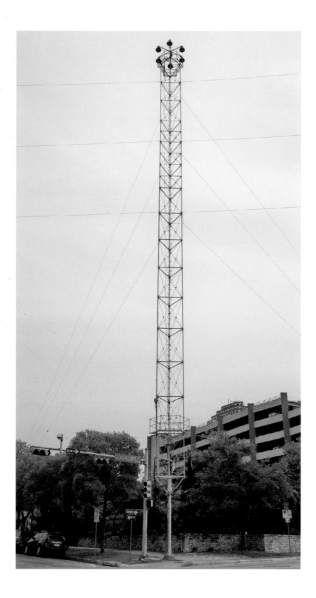

ABOVE: One of the remaining moonlight towers at the southeast corner of Gaudalupe Street and West Ninth Street.

ABOVE: Austin is the only city in the nation that still uses its network of moonlight towers. The lights have seen continuous use and are a quaint curiosity. They even look brand-new. In 1993 the city invested $1.3 million in a ground-up restoration of the remaining towers: taking them apart, replacing components, and repainting. Seventeen are still extant, scattered around town in their original condition—save for the small plaque from the Texas Historical Commission. At Christmastime, the moonlight tower in Zilker Park does double duty as the city's Christmas tree; its guy wires host thousands of tiny lights. Like many local legends, the lights have spawned urban myths, such as their placement citywide being in the shape of a star or their activation originally causing chickens to lay eggs twenty-four hours a day (neither of which are true).

c.1920

THE ALAMO, SAN ANTONIO

Site of the siege that inspired Texans to inflict a crushing defeat on Mexico

ABOVE: The Alamo came to national prominence after the 1836 battle in which the Mexican forces of General Santa Anna besieged rebelling Texas citizens. What we call the Alamo today was originally the San Antonio de Valero mission, chartered by the Mexican viceroy in 1716 to educate local natives and convert them to Christianity. *Alamo* is Spanish for cottonwood, which is found in nearby groves. Santa Anna mounted a massive assault and slaughtered the Texan rebels after a thirteen-day siege. The Alamo wasn't a strategically important location for either side in a strictly martial sense; there was no critical bridge, vital port, or cache of resources. For the Mexican military, it was about controlling a rebellion. And for the Texans (many of whom were ethnic Mexicans), it was about creating a new nation. Both sides were trying to prove a point—which they both did. Inspired by the stand of Jim Bowie and William Travis, the settlers defeated the Mexicans at the Battle of San Jacinto later that year and took control of their own destiny.

ABOVE: After the Battle of the Alamo, the Republic of Texas passed an act returning the grounds to the church in 1841. When the United States annexed Texas, it demanded ownership—then turned around and leased it to the church. In 1905 the state legislature granted ownership to the Daughters of the Republic of Texas. It is a popular tourist spot, with 2.5 million visitors annually. Part museum, part monument, and part cultural icon—visiting the Alamo is always free of charge. The site includes a shrine, as well as multiple educational exhibits on the Texas Revolution and Texas history. Staying true to its pioneering Texas ideals, the Daughters of the Republic of Texas receive no government money whatsoever for managing and maintaining it, relying strictly on private fund-raising and gift shop sales to stay financially self-reliant.

c.1970

BEXAR COUNTY COURTHOUSE
The oldest continuously operating courthouse in the state of Texas

LEFT: At the turn of the twentieth century, San Antonio was the biggest city in Texas, having reached critical mass via cattle, railroads, military facilities, and an influx of settlers from the Southern states. That meant a busy courthouse. The cornerstone for this Romanesque Revival–style beauty, made of native Texas granite and red sandstone, was laid in 1892. J. Riely Gordon, who designed over seventy courthouses, served as the architect. Gordon wanted to make sure that the building would function well in San Antonio's warm climate, so its open court on the east side, facing Dwyer Avenue, was designed to catch the prevailing southeast breeze. He also designed a fountain above the granite steps, columns, and balustrade to create a cooling effect as one entered. Many people think Gordon put forth extra effort in designing it, with its tall tower and colonnades, because he had lived in San Antonio as a boy.

c.1970

RIGHT: Today, the Bexar County Courthouse and the main plaza before it look as splendid as ever. With all of the modern conveniences, it doesn't catch much of a prevailing breeze unless the door is held open. The courtyard fountain out front is more for relaxation than for staying cool. But over 100 years of service has only heightened this grand old building's character. In 1915 a five-story addition to the building's south side was completed, the first of many additions and renovations over the years. The building is still the hub of a busy populace. Not only is San Antonio the seventh-largest city in the United States, but a recent oil and gas boom in the Eagle Ford shale has meant new economic growth in the region. Many of the world's largest energy companies have flocked to the area. The Bexar County Courthouse is the largest and oldest continuously operating historic courthouse in the state of Texas.

ALAMEDA THEATER, SAN ANTONIO

A cinema gem that preservationists are determined to revive

LEFT: Here we see the extravagant Alameda Theater at 318 West Houston Street in 1955. When it opened in March 1949, it was the largest movie palace in America dedicated to Spanish-language cinema and live theater. Its pedigree makes sense given that the historic Casa de Mexico International Building, to which the theater was attached, was also home to the Mexican consulate, as well as the first Mexican chamber of commerce in the United States. The project was the brainchild of San Antonio businessman Tano Lucchese. At its opening, Lucchese proclaimed, "The Alameda will be a permanent symbol of good faith and understanding between the Latin American and Anglo American where they might share and recognize two different cultures." The theater's eighty-six-foot-high marquee lit up the warm San Antonio nights, with more than 1,000 cold cathode lighting elements. Inside, the theater was state-of-the-art, with an Altec sound system, Bodiform chairs, and intricate murals.

RIGHT: By the early 1990s, the theater was in a sad state. For many, the theater's decline was especially painful given the institution's legacy as an icon for Latino culture in the United States. In 1996 its Museo Alameda made an affiliation with the Smithsonian Museum, but that initiative struggled financially. Driven by the desire to protect this rich cultural landmark, a group of intrepid preservationists formed a nonprofit organization and spearheaded the theater's restoration. Through corporate donations and public funds, the theater is on target to undergo $14.3 million in renovations, including doubling the size of the stage, building a mezzanine gallery, and widening the seats to make them more comfortable for patrons. When completed, the theater will help to better tell the American Latino story in a way that only the Alameda could. The "Support Revive Alameda" signage encourages supporters to go online and make donations to help restore the wonderful old theater.

SAN ANTONIO RIVER

At one point, the city was thinking of burying the river under a layer of concrete

1941

LEFT: Native Americans had used the spring-fed waters of the San Antonio River for thousands of years, but it first got the name we know when a group of Spaniards came through the area in 1691. They were camping out by the river on the day of Saint Anthony of Padua, and christened it San Antonio de Padua. When the Spanish set up their missions, they used it for irrigation. By the 1890s, water wells were dug into the underground aquifer around the region—slowing the flow of the spring-fed river considerably. But by the early 1900s, it flooded so many times that the city threatened to lay down concrete and turn it into a sewer. To prevent further flooding, the Olmos Dam was constructed in 1926. Just a few years later, a young architect named Robert H. H. Hugman came up with a crazy idea. He wanted to add a floodgate and an adjustable weir to the river downtown—shutting the river off to potential flooding, and at the same time allowing a surge of commercial development at the river level. What would be known as the San Antonio River Walk was all Hugman's idea. He was inspired by the old cities in Spain, with their narrow, winding streets and intricate features—pedestrian traffic only. By the time it was dedicated in 1941, Works Progress Administration funds had been used to add 17,000 feet of new sidewalk, thirty-one stairways, more than 4,000 trees and plants, and other features.

RIGHT: The River Walk is synonymous with the city itself and draws visitors worldwide to spend a hot afternoon sipping a salted margarita in the shade of a great oak tree by the lazy river. A favorite pastime for visitors is taking a river tour. The water is about four feet deep, and it is drained every other year for maintenance—and to gather the random collection of tourists' personal belongings that have fallen in. Robert Hugman is celebrated in the inscription on the balustrade that overlooks the grandest of his many civic projects.

c.1970

FORT SAM HOUSTON, SAN ANTONIO

"In Peace Prepare for War"

LEFT: After the annexation of Texas, the U.S. Army began to establish outposts in San Antonio. Various temporary forces and facilities were installed, but a major base wasn't begun until after the Civil War. The city donated ninety-three acres, on which the Edward Braden Construction Company built the quadrangle shown here. The ninety-foot-tall tower was commenced in 1876 to house a water tank. A clock was installed in 1882, replaced in 1907 by the one we see today. There is a stone inscription commemorating the building of the quadrangle at the top: "Erected by an Act of Congress, 1877. In Peace Prepare for War." Expansion began forthwith. A depot, officers' quarters, hospital, and the 10,830-square-foot commander's house went up almost immediately. Geronimo, the famed war chief of the Bedonkohe Apache, was held here for a brief time before being exiled. By the time the base got its official name in 1890, sixty new buildings had gone up.

1905

ABOVE: Soldiers drill on the grounds of Fort Sam Houston in 1905 prior to a visit by President Theodore Roosevelt.

1918

BELOW: The quadrangle looks much the same today. After World War I, the base grew exponentially, with hundreds of new buildings and countless specialized military units. "Fort Sam" is a vital part of San Antonio's culture. All kinds of units work at the base, from military intelligence to the United States Fifth Army. The quadrangle may look the same, but the base has since grown into a significant provider of a critical military capacity: health care. The base spent $3 million on a hospital in the mid-1930s and has been adding health-care expertise and infrastructure ever since. It's home to the U.S. Army's Health Services Command, the Brooke Army Medical Center, the Academy of Health Services, the U.S. Army Dental Laboratory, and the Institute of Surgical Research. Almost 30,000 military and civilian personnel work at Fort Sam, and the base gets bigger and better every year.

LEFT: The entrance gate in 1918 as troops mobilized for World War I.

c.1929

STINSON FIELD, SAN ANTONIO
Named after a family of remarkable aviation pioneers

ABOVE: This photograph shows San Antonio's original airfield on Mission Road, sometime between 1927 and 1931. Stinson Field was San Antonio's first municipal airport. The facility was named after the prominent Stinson family of aviators. It opened in 1915 and has been in continuous operation ever since. The Stinsons were a colorful lot; they took up flying when it was still a novel affair. Katherine Stinson was taught to fly by one of the Wright brothers' pilots and flew exhibitions, specializing in a loop-the-loop maneuver. She was America's fourth licensed female pilot (her sister, Marjorie, was the ninth). Her brother Eddie was also a stunt pilot and formed the Stinson Aircraft Company. The family ran a flying school at Fort Sam Houston before leasing land from the city to start the airport. For nine years, including during the time this picture was taken, the airport was named Winburn Field after reporter Bill Winburn, who died in a plane crash.

ABOVE: During World War I and after, the airport ceased to be a private affair and was run by the City of San Antonio. In 1936 a new terminal (right) was completed as part of the Works Progress Administration program. During World War II, the military used the facility as a training base—and built over a hundred buildings on the site (only a few remain). Today, Stinson is the second-oldest continually used airport in the United States. The place is still hopping with oilmen flying private jets, recreational pilots taking toys for a spin, regional air carriers shuttling Texans hither and yon—as well as a fair amount of helicopter traffic. In 2008 a major terminal expansion was completed, adding 24,000 square feet, though the original terminal was left intact. The old tower in the middle of the picture is still used as Stinson's control tower today.

LEFT: Katherine Stinson pictured on a trip to Japan in 1917, the same year she set a new American nonstop record, flying 606 miles from San Diego to San Francisco. On the flying exhibition circuit, she was dubbed "the flying schoolgirl" even though she was twenty-one years old. The Stinson School in San Antonio did not last out World War I, and Katherine then became a Red Cross ambulance driver in Europe. She died in 1977 at the age of eighty-six.

c.1927

LEFT: The Scottish Rite Cathedral on the southeast corner of Avenue E and Fourth Street, around 1927. The Scottish Rite is a Masonic organization (a fraternal group with roots in medieval stonemasons). The Classic Revival building was only three years old at this time. Its authoritative Corinthian columns, elaborate bronze work, and gabled front portico give it a true air of authority. Freemasons have been active in Texas since the years of the republic. Almost all of the founding fathers of Texas, from Sam Houston and Stephen F. Austin to Alamo heroes Jim Bowie and Davy Crockett, were Masons. Although the building is called a cathedral, Freemasonry isn't a religion, and most Scottish Rite Masons are not Scottish—the practice actually originated in France. The cathedral cost $1.5 million when it was built in 1924.

RIGHT: While the building cost $1.5 million, it wasn't paid for up front. In fact, the organization was racked with debts over its construction for decades to come. When the building was completed, the Masons still owed around $900,000. They struggled, and the great stock market crash and subsequent Depression only made it worse. But the group finally paid it off, free and clear, by the early 1950s. It was placed on the National Register of Historic Places in 1996. Today, the Scottish Rite Cathedral still serves as the headquarters for the Scottish Rite Masons in San Antonio. It is not only a Masonic lodge but also a library and museum, and is available for rent as a banquet/meeting venue. The Masons still play a big part in Texas culture. With 890 lodges and 105,000 members, the Grand Lodge of Texas is the fifth-largest Masonic grand lodge in the world. Most of their activities involve volunteerism and acts of philanthropy.

SCOTTISH RITE CATHEDRAL, SAN ANTONIO
The building was so grand it took thirty years to pay the construction bill

RIGHT: A detail of the grand Greek Revival building. Scottish Rite Masonry in San Antonio dates to 1912; the organization obtained the site for their temple in 1919. The building was started in 1922 and finished two years later. A feature of the building is the elaborately sculpted bronze doors by artist Pompeo Coppini.

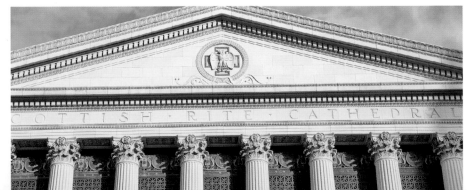

c.1930

MENGER HOTEL, SAN ANTONIO

Serving visitors and pilgrims to San Antonio since the time of the Alamo siege

ABOVE: A longtime San Antonio fixture, the hotel is named for William Menger, a German immigrant who opened a brewery and boardinghouse on this spot at Alamo Square in the early 1840s. Menger wanted to expand the boardinghouse, and the hotel was the result of his efforts. It was so successful he had yet another addition built between the brewery and hotel (a secret tunnel connected the two). By the time Menger passed away in 1871, the

Menger Hotel was the most famous hotel in the Southwest. Its colonial dining room was known for delicacies such as mango ice cream, wild game, and snapper soup made from San Antonio River turtles. Robert E. Lee was staying there when he decided to fight for the Confederacy, and President Theodore Roosevelt stayed at the Menger while on hunting trips.

ABOVE: The Menger is the undisputed grand dame of historic Texas hotels—the oldest continuously operating hotel west of the Mississippi. An east wing was added in 1881. In 1887 its owners installed an opulent bar made of solid cherry wood, a replica of the one at the House of Lords Club in London. The bar became famous for its mint juleps, and for the cold beer chilled by the Alamo Madre ditch passing through the hotel's courtyard. In 1909 architect Alfred Giles designed yet another addition—altering the building's facade and adding a breathtaking rotunda inside. The Great Depression wasn't kind to the hotel, but over the years it's been stunningly restored. Yet another wing was added in 1951, along with a massive modernization project by architect Atlee B. Ayres, the official state architect at the time. With fine amenities such as a lobby rich with historic accoutrements to a splendid Sunday champagne brunch, many Texans consider it the best place to stay in San Antonio.

1942

RODD FIELD / CUDDIHY FIELD, CORPUS CHRISTI

Two of the many satellite airfields that helped make Corpus Christi the navy's biggest pilot training facility in World War II

1942

1942

ABOVE: Seaplanes photographed in Corpus Christi, August 1942. Seaplanes played a big role in World War II not only as training aircraft but also as effective tactical tools for antisubmarine warfare, reconnaissance, and search-and-rescue missions.

ABOVE: Cadets work on a Vought OS2U Kingfisher seaplane at Corpus Christi in August 1942. The Kingfisher had a large central float and two outer stabilizing floats.

FAR LEFT: This 1942 photo of Rodd Field, one of the naval air station's auxiliary airfields, shows it buzzing with Allied air traffic. The government bought this 861-acre patch of land just southwest of Corpus Christi in 1940. In this image can be seen two of the field's three massive hangars, and training planes of all types. The facility had four runways, two circular landing areas, and a number of outlying fields. The attack on Pearl Harbor threw the navy's activity in and around Corpus Christi into overdrive. By 1944, it was the world's largest naval aviation training facility. It covered 20,000 acres and sported 997 hangars, barracks, and other buildings. Six satellite airfields—Cabaniss, Cuddihy, Chase, Kingsville, Rodd, and Waldron Fields—supported the main base. Throughout the war it cranked out 35,000 naval pilots, including future president George H. W. Bush, who was in the third graduating class in June 1943. In the 1950s, the base was the home of the Blue Angels.

ABOVE: Following the war, many of NAS Corpus Christi's auxiliary airfields were sold, abandoned, or decommissioned. Rodd Field outlived the war but was shut down in the 1950s. Portions of the large facility were sold to private concerns, and some on the north end of the property to NASA for the Texas Manned Space Flight Network Tracking Station. That facility was closed in the early 1970s. By 1980 only one hangar—and none of the runways—remained. That year, the city built Bill Wilt Park on a portion of the land. Cuddihy Field (pictured) was closed shortly after World War II, and became a civil airport in 1947. The runways were abandoned by the 1960s, and by 2005 one dilapidated hangar and a single runway remained at the site. Today, the main base at NAS Corpus Christi is home to the Chief of Naval Air Training, Training Air Wing 4, the Marine Aviation Training Support Group, and several other aviation, fleet, and logistical commands.

c.1930

THE BLUFF, CORPUS CHRISTI
Marking the upper and lower levels of Corpus Christi

ABOVE: This photo was taken in the 1930s, overlooking the street ramp that led to Upper Broadway. Corpus Christi was originally a coastal trading post; first for Native Americans and later for a man named Henry Kinney. Kinney chose this high ground as a location for his business. Ever since, it's been considered choice land and the city has been divided between the Bluff (the upper part of the city) and the beach that lies below. This spot between Upper and Lower Broadway has always been considered the Bluff's ground zero. The land below the Bluff was always flooding, making the streets connecting the two slippery. In 1912 Mayor Roy Miller led an effort to beautify the Bluff. In the following years, it was terraced and leveled and equipped with retaining walls—plus a beautiful balustrade with stairways. Here, one can see the Federal Building on the left and the gardens of the Plaza Hotel on the right.

ABOVE: The Plaza Hotel is gone, but what is now the Wells Fargo Building still stands (with Leopard Street and Upper Broadway to the right). Over the years, the Bluff has seen a lot of expansion. Six stairways connect Upper and Lower Broadway. The Grand Staircase is at People's Street. At its bottom is a sculpture honoring the area's Confederate veterans. Created by Pompeo Coppini, the statue depicts Father Neptune and Mother Earth crowning Corpus Christi "Queen of the Sea." In 1931 the park was expanded to create Spohn Park, on the opposite side of the Bluff. The park features a World War I memorial composed of a lollipop-like gold star and markers in remembrance of fallen servicemen. In 1988 the Bluff was listed in the National Register of Historic Places. The former Federal Building with the red tile roof houses the offices of the Thomas J. Henry Injury Attorneys firm.

c.1935

CENTENNIAL HOUSE, CORPUS CHRISTI
A home that has withstood time, hurricanes, Yankee gunships, and Mexican bandits

ABOVE: Also known as the Britton-Evans House, this grand Greek Revival structure was built in 1849 by Forbes Britton. Britton fought in the Mexican War, made money in shipping, and served in the state senate. He wasn't a man of half-measures, and he built the house to last. It is made of "shellcrete," which consisted of crushed seashells, lime, and water—three layers of this brick were covered by plaster. During the Civil War, the well-built structure served as a war hospital when Yankee gunships pounded the city. It was used as a shelter when Mexican bandits raided Corpus Christi in a violent crime spree in 1875. And it made a great storm shelter in hurricanes that blew through town over the decades. Britton passed on in 1861. George Evans, who would go on to become mayor, purchased the house in 1880 and lived there until 1936. It then became the headquarters of the Southern Mineral Company.

ABOVE: Wedged between a massive AT&T building, the Corpus Christi Cathedral next door, and other downtown commercial buildings, the Britton-Evans House doesn't impose itself on the landscape as it once did. But it's still the oldest building in Corpus Christi in its original spot. It's also the oldest house between San Antonio and Laredo. It was renamed Centennial House in 1949. The Southern Mineral Company did a fine job of maintaining the house, but the company moved out in the 1960s. The Corpus Christi Heritage Society stepped in, purchasing and restoring the property—then opening it to the public. The house was added to the National Register of Historic Places in 1976. In 2002 the building underwent a $500,000 repair and waterproofing job where the shellcrete had been beaten down by over 150 years of service. Visitors today can still appreciate the sturdy construction of the house, as well as its bay-facing view.

1943

USS *LEXINGTON*, CORPUS CHRISTI

The Japanese nicknamed the ship "the Blue Ghost"

ABOVE: This ship was to be named the *Cabot*, but at the last minute it was renamed the *Lexington* in honor of the battleship that was lost during the Battle of the Coral Sea in 1942; it was the seventh U.S. Navy vessel to bear the name. An Essex-class aircraft carrier, the *Lexington* was built in Quincy, Massachusetts, and commissioned in 1943. The *Lexington* initially joined the Fifth Fleet at Pearl Harbor, and would eventually touch almost every major operation in the Pacific Theater. Japanese propagandists nicknamed the ship "the Blue Ghost"

because of its distinctive dark blue camouflage and its penchant for seeming to rise from the dead—it was reported as having been sunk at least four times. It was struck by kamikaze suicide planes, it burned, and it was the subject of constant gunfire. Yet the *Lexington* kept coming back—dispatching 847 enemy planes, destroying over 900,000 tons of enemy cargo, and laying waste to Japanese military positions all across the Pacific.

1943

ABOVE: Aboard the aircraft carrier USS *Lexington*, flight deck crewmen spot a pair of Douglas SBD-5 Scout Bombers at the aft end of the flight deck, in preparation for takeoff in 1943. An F6F-3 Hellcat fighter is parked farther forward.

BELOW: The crew of the USS *Lexington* stands at attention for a burial at sea while en route to New Guinea on April 2, 1944. The plane at left is a Grumman F6F-5 Hellcat.

1944

ABOVE: Today the *Lexington* serves as the USS Lexington Museum on the Bay. It is a self-funded naval aviation museum that has entertained and educated millions of area residents and tourists through its exhibits, theater, and the experience of getting a behind-the-scenes look at a World War II aircraft carrier. For its service in the war, the *Lexington* received the Presidential Unit Citation. When the war ended, it was decommissioned and sent to Bremerton, Washington, for upgrades. It hit the water again in 1955, serving a number of roles before eventually becoming a training carrier in the Gulf of Mexico. When it was finally donated to Corpus Christi in 1992, it was the last of the Essex-class carriers. The ship became a National Historic Landmark in 2003. Its distinctive blue hull is lit at night, and can be seen for miles around. The plane on the left is an A-6E Intruder; on the right is an F/A-18 Hornet that once flew with the Blue Angels.

1934

PORT ISABEL LIGHTHOUSE, CORPUS CHRISTI

Dark for over a century, yet visitors still come for the view

LEFT: In the mid-1800s, sea captains passing along the southeastern coast of Texas often complained of its hard-to-navigate coastline. In response, the U.S. government built this brick lighthouse in 1852. Standing fifty-seven feet high, its light could be seen for sixteen miles. Not only did this help commercial sailors navigate the area, it also became an important military asset for the region. During the Civil War, the lighthouse became an observation tower for both sides at various times. While the tower was under Confederate control, John "Rip" Ford ordered that its light and lens be buried so that invading Yankees couldn't make use of the light. Nobody ever found them, but the parts were replaced in 1866. In the 1880s, the lighthouse received a number of upgrades, but in 1888 the lights were turned off. It was proven that the U.S. government didn't actually have the title to the land, so the operation of the lighthouse ceased.

c.1940

RIGHT: When the government got the proper title of the land in 1895, the lighthouse was back in business. But soon it had another problem: obsolescence. Newer, bigger towers went up. In 1905 the U.S. government shut it down, and later sold the lighthouse and the land in 1927, after which the Great Depression made the prospect of operation difficult. It received a state historical marker in 1936—and helped locals keep an eye out for German submarines during World War II. In the 1950s, its owners donated the facility to the state for historical preservation; today it serves as the Port Isabel Lighthouse State Historic Site— sitting on a scenic patch of coastal grass that's perfect for a picnic. On any given weekend one can find couples getting married at the top, photographers shooting its vintage architecture, or beachgoers taking in the view. It takes seventy-five winding steps and three short ladders to reach the top. The carefully preserved Lighthouse Keeper's Cottage is also worth a visit.

c.1928

DOWNTOWN CORPUS CHRISTI

Only the Ritz Theatre is left from the 1920s, but is awaiting refurbishment

ABOVE: This photo shows Chaparral Street in downtown Corpus Christi, circa 1928, just before the Great Depression. In 1926 the city opened its new deepwater port and Corpus Christi was bouncing back from the hurricane of 1919. On the left can be seen Nueces Shoe Repairing, which could fix or clean just about anything. Next door at 412 North Chaparral was the Faust Café, which was started by the Lymberry family. Long and narrow, it sported a lunch counter and private tables—and looked like a grand old caricature of a diner

from the 1920s (the oysters were popular). To the right were the offices of cotton broker Ed Smith. Today, people think of the oil business, chemicals, and manufacturing when they think of the Corpus Christi shipping trade. But back in the early days of the port, cotton was king, and a number of people made their living as cotton brokers. The Ritz Theatre is shown at the far right.

ABOVE: These days, downtown is a lot more developed than it used to be. And while this strip of buildings is still in the thick of it all, some are starting to show their age. Many of the original business tenants in the area are gone. Today, Grandma Lira Mexican Food and other retail shops occupy the building where the shoe repairmen once worked. What was once the office of the cotton broker now houses Dr. Rockit's Blues Bar and Carl's Fine Flowers, which

delivers all over town. The Ritz Theatre, which had a decades-long run as a glamorous movie house, fizzled as a theater in the early 1970s. It housed a number of entertainment-focused businesses in the following years, but ceased operations in the 1980s. Its screens have been dark for years, but a big push is currently underway by a nonprofit organization to restore the old theater.

NORTH BEACH, CORPUS CHRISTI

The souvenir stands may be gone, but the beach is still a popular destination

BELOW: North Beach refers to the beach north of the Harbor Bridge, a longtime popular tourist destination. This shot of its main drag was taken in 1939 (the Highway 77/181 sign can be seen on the right). North Beach was the place to be for sun and sand at the time. In 1919 a devastating hurricane blew through the area, killing hundreds of people and leaving only three buildings standing. It took years for the area to bounce back, but it rebounded with a vengeance. By the time this picture was taken, the party was back in full swing. Up and down this road were shops to buy beer and groceries for a big day out at the beach. Many say North Beach peaked in the 1930s and 1940s, when it offered all kinds of tourist attractions, including a boardwalk, an amusement park, a Ferris wheel, swimsuit contests, a diving platform, a water slide, dancing, restaurants, icehouses, and ice-cream parlors.

1939

1939

LEFT: Tourist shops at North Beach, Corpus Christi, photographed by Farm Security Administration photographer Russell Lee in February 1939. The area was a tourist destination and also housed many of the workers constructing the U.S. Navy stations around town.

BELOW: These hotels house the same types of beachgoers their predecessors catered to so many years ago. North Beach has the beach as well as the USS *Lexington* and the Texas State Aquarium—not to mention popular beachside restaurants such as Fajitaville. It's been a rocky road, though. When the Harbor Bridge was completed in 1959, visitors started to bypass the area. To promote the beach, the city began marketing it as "Corpus Christi Beach." Only the residents still knew it as North Beach. But this only confused people, so in 2012 the city officially reverted back to the North Beach name. It still offers great family beaches, and the recently installed granite markers every tenth of a mile make it popular for runners and walkers. Campers, surfers, sailboarders, and office workers looking for a little sunshine flock to North Beach daily. In 2012 it received the Best Restored Beach Award from the American Shore and Beach Preservation Association.

1936

MISSION ESPÍRITU SANTO DE ZÚÑIGA, GOLIAD
The mission holds a place in Texas history almost as significant as the Alamo

LEFT: Mission Nuestra Señora del Espíritu Santo de Zúñiga was established by the Spaniards in what was then New Spain, to convert native Karankawa Indians to Christianity. It was moved a few times, finally to La Bahia, which is now Goliad. Many referred to the mission as La Bahia. Shown here is not the actual presidio but its mission and chapel. The mission was a prosperous one for many decades. When Mexico declared independence from Spain, its funding was cut under Mexican rule. The Franciscans looked after it as long as they could despite this lack of support. The facility's presidio grounds are infamous for the Goliad Massacre. After an unsuccessful campaign in the Texas Revolution, the Mexican army captured hundreds of Texan prisoners and held them in the La Bahia presidio. Mexican military leader General Antonio Lopez de Santa Anna had each man executed (as many as 407 by some counts). This photo was taken a hundred years later, in 1936.

BELOW: The southeast elevation of what is also known as La Bahia presidio.

1936

ABOVE: The mission was carefully reconstructed by a Civil Conservation Corps initiative in the 1930s. When word spread of Santa Anna's actions, the Texas revolutionaries merely fought harder. During the Battle of San Jacinto, soldiers shouted "Remember the Alamo!" and "Remember Goliad!" as they struck down their enemies. After the war, the Republic of Texas passed ownership of the mission back to the Catholic Church. In 1931 the State of Texas assumed ownership. A number of restoration and research projects were performed at the site, many of which were funded by New Deal legislation. Today, it is part of the Goliad State Historical Park. Tours of the restored mission are offered, and visitors can also see the Fannin Memorial where the fallen Texan revolutionaries are buried. In the larger Goliad State Park complex, one can also go hiking, fishing, swimming, or bird-watching along part of the Great Texas Coastal Birding Trail.

c.1900

ALLEN'S LANDING, HOUSTON

Where the founders of Houston are believed to have come ashore and started their grand plan

ABOVE: This photo shows what is now known as Allen's Landing, back in the early days of Houston when it was a burgeoning commercial hub. This is actually Houston's old port, which sat at the confluence of the White Oak and Buffalo Bayous. August C. Allen and John K. Allen, brothers from New York with a flair for real-estate development, founded the city of Houston. During the republic years, starting in 1836, the Allens saw an opportunity to create a great "center of government and commerce" from scratch (and then rake in huge profits as it grew along with the young nation). They purchased the land and named the new city after Republic of Texas hero and president Sam Houston. Allen's Landing is said to be the spot where they first came ashore to begin their new empire. The paddleboat shown here was called the *St. Claire*; the S. L. Allen Company building is in the background on the left.

ABOVE: While the Republic of Texas didn't last, the city of Houston did. It is the fourth-largest city in the United States, and one of the largest ports. With the construction of the ship channel, the old port saw much less trade—though it was still at the heart of downtown. The City of Houston Parks and Recreation Department bought the land in 1966. It is now a developed urban greenscape that pays homage to Houston's founders and also gives Houston urbanites a place to kayak, walk, view public art exhibits, or just kick back under the shade of an oak tree. Millions of dollars have been invested into improving the 1.76-acre spot, which comes ashore at 1001 Commerce Street. On the left side of this photo is the former Merchants and Manufacturers Building at One Main, now the University of Houston Downtown. The building on the right is the Harris County Jail.

RIGHT: This public art installation adorns a terrace overlooking the landing; the sound of water passes by below. It reads: "The sound of water says what I think. Water fountains water colors water dreams water worlds water garden water falls."

c.1900

CONGRESS AVENUE, HOUSTON
Changing from small stores and free enterprise to grand civic governance

ABOVE: The quaint turn-of-the-century retail stores lining Congress Avenue around Fannin Street show early Houston's enterprising spirit. The roads might not have been paved, but the path to prosperity was cleared by a laissez-faire attitude of building something from nothing. Dry-goods stores, hoards of book dealers, launderers, furniture stores, druggists, and more were fueling Houstonians with the basics needed to help bring Texas to the forefront of American prosperity. This was a time of transformation; horse-drawn carriages and bowler hats mixed with the electric railcars rattling down the tracks in the center of the street. The store on the far right specialized in dry goods, books, stationery, and clothes. One can just make out the banner on the store to its left, which reads "Racket Store." That was what the old-timers used to call a five-and-dime or small variety shop. Land deals, shoot-outs, idle gossip, political scheming, new inventions, and risky business ventures all happened here.

60

ABOVE: The scenery on Congress Avenue has changed a lot. The distinctive old Victorian Sweeney, Coombs, and Fredericks Building at Congress and Main is still around. But on this stretch of Congress, all of the old charming bookstores and five-and-dimes have met the wrecking ball. These days, government agencies representing state, county, local, and federal organizations identified by acronyms occupy blocks upon blocks of Congress Street; the county bought part of it. The beautiful 1910 courthouse is seen on the right; it just received a $65 million, five-year restoration. A huge family law center building with a small green space is on the left, just out of the photo. The Harris County Civil Court Building looms in the distance on the left. There's not a lot of free enterprise going on in this particular spot, unless you count taxes or lawyer's fees. But one thing is for sure: not many drivers speed through this part of town.

c.1905

OLD COTTON EXCHANGE, HOUSTON

Once a staple of the Texas economy, cotton is still grown, but the need for an exchange has long since passed

ABOVE: Even in the early twentieth century, when this photo was taken, commodity traders couldn't help showing off their cars in front of the exchange. Back in the day, oil didn't run Houston—cotton did. It was a huge part of the Texas economy prior to World War II. Even the Spanish missionaries who predated Anglo-American settlement of the region produced thousands of pounds every year. The Houston Cotton Exchange Building was used by the Houston Board of Trade to establish standards and pricing that ensured fair trade and classification of cotton. Architect Eugene T. Heiner, who also designed many buildings at Texas A&M University, toured several exchange buildings before putting pen to paper. His redbricked Classical Revival design at the corner of Franklin and Travis originally had only three floors. The fourth floor was added in 1907 during renovation and remodeling. By 1924 the exchange had outgrown the building. The new exchange building, at Franklin and Caroline, sported the cornerstone from this building in its lobby.

ABOVE: After World War II, cotton production in Texas declined, and also shifted from the eastern and southeastern part of the state to the south and west. The crop-destroying boll weevil came up from Mexico and eventually spread across Texas and the whole American South, devastating cotton crops. Foreign production, synthetic fibers, and increasing urbanization of Texas lands meant a shifting landscape for the cotton market. Today's Texas cotton farms are fewer in number and highly mechanized. The Houston Cotton Exchange and Board of Trade disbanded shortly after its hundredth year. The old exchange building was restored and reconfigured into office space in 1971. So while people in today's Houston may not think twice about cotton, they do take a second look when passing the old Cotton Exchange Building. Today, it's a stylish property that hosts offices for Houston criminal defense attorney Joe Wells and several other law firms and businesses, and also houses a bar.

c.1940

CITY HALL, HOUSTON

The mayor at the time thought his new building was too fancy by half

ABOVE: Houston's city hall was completed in 1939. Prior to the construction of this building (which took just twenty months), the city's legal affairs were handled in the city hall off Market Square. When this building was finished, the old city hall was turned into a bus terminal that later burned down. This building cost $1,670,000 to build—45 percent of which was covered by Works Progress Administration funds. Joseph Finger served as architect for the "ultra-modern" building. The mayor at the time, R. H. Fonville, hated the design and never missed an opportunity to say so (he'd wanted architect A. C. Finn to get the job). Fonville thought it was too fancy, quipping that he wanted something "for the masses, not the classes."

c.1900

ABOVE: City Hall's predecessor at the turn of the twentieth century.

RIGHT: The old city hall still looks modern and sleek, but it couldn't possibly handle the level of city affairs handled by the city's administrators. The Houston government alone these days has over 500 buildings and 23,000 employees. But the city hall still has a lot of presence, despite the massive city that's grown up around it. The mayor still has offices in the building, which originally offered a private elevator, showers, and "escape route" passageways so that public servants could dodge pesky taxpayers. All of the building's adornments, including the reflecting pool and friezes depicting the industries of Houston, are just as beautiful as when originally crafted. If you want to take Houston's political pulse or just find something interesting to do, stand in front of the city hall on any given day, and you are bound to come across a variety of charity events, public speakers, and protesters.

UNION STATION AND THE TEXAS ROCKET, HOUSTON

The rockets have departed, but the Astros have arrived to take their place

LEFT: The heart of Houston transportation for generations, Union Station was built in 1911 at Crawford Street and Texas Avenue. The grand, three-story train station was designed by the architectural firm of Warren & Wetmore (who also designed the Grand Central Terminal and the Ritz-Carlton in New York City). Union Station was part of a $5 million downtown train terminal and warehouse complex that brought together multiple railways via thirteen tracks. The building boasted a main hall with grand columns and arches featuring a lunch counter and the Harvey House dining room—an upscale franchise restaurant throughout the West. The Harvey House served the original "blue plate special," served on a blue china plate. As Houston grew, the building saw more traffic. More floors were added later. This shot was taken around 1928. The shiny futuristic train (below) was the Texas Rocket, which ran from Houston to Fort Worth from 1937 to 1945.

c.1928

1938

ABOVE: Throughout the United States, passenger rail declined in the late 1960s and early 1970s. Union Station couldn't buck the trend. In the mid-1970s, it halted services, and remaining industrial rail service trickled off to other random connections. Abandoned in a now-underdeveloped section of east downtown Houston, it seemed doomed. What would save it? Of all things: baseball. The Houston Astros had been shopping for a new venue—and decided it would be a good idea to build on the old Union Station. The result

was a beautiful restoration and reconstruction; the Astros made the old train station part of their new ballpark. In 2000 it was christened Enron Field after its primary corporate sponsor. Following the high-profile and scandalous derailment of Enron, the stadium was rededicated as Minute Maid Park. The Texas Rocket was replaced in 1945 by the Twin Star Rocket, which ran from Houston to Minneapolis–St. Paul.

c.1920

RICE UNIVERSITY, HOUSTON

The prestigious academic institution should have been celebrating its centenary long before 2012

ABOVE: William Marsh Rice University had been established for only a few years when this photo was taken in the 1920s. Herzstein Hall is seen on the left, and Lovett Hall on the right. Rice, a wealthy Houston merchant, chartered the school in 1891 for "the advancement of literature, science, and art." The school didn't open until 1912, however, after much intrigue on the part of the Rice estate. William Marsh Rice funded the school via interest-bearing notes and other vehicles payable upon his death. However, Rice's personal lawyer

and his butler decided that his estate would be better served if it were made payable to the two of them personally. To expedite payment, they murdered Rice via chloroform in 1900. By the time the scheme was revealed and the estate rightly settled in 1904, the money set aside for the school's founding had grown to more than $3.3 million. Edgar Odell Lovett, a Princeton astronomer and mathematician, served as Rice University's first president.

Herzstein Hall and Lovett Hall have retained their elegant appearance. The upside of the Rice murder debacle meant that his funds accumulated over the years, providing the school with quite a war chest. In fact, no student accepted into the academically exclusive university had to pay any tuition at all—a dynamic that stayed in effect until 1965. Today, Rice is one of the nation's leading universities—and one of the world's top fifty universities. It is a powerhouse scientific research center, and a higher percentage of its students receive National Science Foundation fellowships than any other American university. Both Herzstein Hall and Lovett Hall are in use today as the physics and administration buildings, respectively. The campus has evolved into an expansive, verdant oasis among Houston's glass and concrete. NASA located what is now its Johnson Space Center complex in Houston partly for access to the big brains at Rice. President John F. Kennedy gave his famous speech justifying America's trip to the moon at the Rice campus.

RIGHT: The grand entrance arch of the administration building, now named Lovett Hall for Edgar Odell Lovett, Rice's first president. Lovett hired architect Ralph Adams Cram to design the building that would ultimately carry his name, as well as many other distinctive buildings on the campus.

c.1950

SHAMROCK HOTEL, HOUSTON

Any color of uniform could be worn, as long as it was green

LEFT: This gargantuan hotel at Main Street and West Holcombe (then called Bellaire Boulevard) was the pinnacle of nouveau riche hospitality in Texas after World War II. Built by wildcat oilman Glen McCarthy between 1946 and 1949, it was the biggest hotel built in the United States during the 1940s. And big was the name of the game in 1946 Houston. Money flowed from the ground, the war was won, and the future was as wide open as a Texas sunset. The eighteen-story building had a green-tiled roof, eighteen different staff uniforms (each a different shade of green), and the world's biggest outdoor swimming pool, which hosted water-skiing exhibitions. At the grand opening on St. Patrick's Day 1949, over 50,000 Houstonians and around 150 Hollywood celebrities attended. *Time* magazine called the party "the most dazzling exhibition of evening dresses and big names ever seen in Texas." The hotel's interior color scheme consisted of sixty-three shades of green—a tribute to McCarthy's Irish heritage.

ABOVE: Swimsuit contests were one way of focusing attention on the Shamrock's enormous swimming pool, seen to the left of the building in the aerial view.

ABOVE: The Shamrock Hotel's parking garage and convention building remain, but today the land is used by the Texas A&M Institute of Biosciences and Technology. As beloved as the Shamrock Hotel was, many local businesspeople had doubts about its financial viability from the start. Its location was an issue; it was quite far from downtown at the time. As Houston's highways developed, they didn't grow in a way favorable to the Shamrock's location. There was no airport nearby and no major business district in the immediate area at the time. McCarthy's fortunes waned in the mid-1950s, and the hotel became part of the Hilton chain. Already on its back foot from low occupancy, the Shamrock's luck ran out when the oil bust of the 1980s came around. It closed in 1986. Hilton donated the building and land to the Texas Medical Center. Demolition of the hotel began in 1987, and today the Shamrock lives on only in legend.

THE ASTRODOME, HOUSTON

The stadium that revolutionized not only baseball but football as well

BELOW: When the Astrodome opened its doors on April 9, 1965, it was hailed as the "Eighth Wonder of the World." It was the world's first multipurpose domed stadium, and paved the way for other domed stadiums elsewhere. It came about as a result of former state representative and Houston mayor Roy Hofheinz's quest to bring a Major League Baseball team to Houston. The league agreed—but only on the condition that Houston build a covered stadium so that people wouldn't be harassed by Houston's giant mosquitoes or suffer from heat strokes in the summer months. Hofheinz raised most of the Astrodome's construction money via public bonds. He would own controlling shares in Houston's new baseball team, called the Colt .45s (later renamed the Astros). He even lobbied Texas road builders to speed up the construction of Loop 610, the thoroughfare running past the stadium. To christen the facility Texas style, the ground was shot with Colt .45 pistols.

1965

ABOVE: The great dome as it looked soon after construction was completed.

1965

BELOW: Today the Astrodome is a part of Reliant Park, which contains not just the Reliant Astrodome but the massive Reliant Stadium seen on the left; it seats more than 71,000 and looms over the dome like something from outer space. A year after opening, the Astrodome became the third most-visited man-made attraction in the nation behind only the Golden Gate Bridge and Mount Rushmore. Compared to today's new norm of high-tech megastadiums, it seems quaint. But it's still the stadium that started it all. It also introduced the world to Astroturf, which was conceived after grass in the dome kept dying from lack of sunlight. Over the years, the Astrodome was expanded to seat around 65,000 fans. After five decades of service, both the ravages of time and the creation of larger facilities have caused the Astrodome to fade from the limelight.

1941

WILLIAM P. HOBBY AIRPORT, HOUSTON

The rapid expansion of the airport soon made the stylish 1940 terminal obsolete

ABOVE: This dashing young lady is shown in 1941 in front of her new flash coupe, a state-of-the-art Douglas DC-3, and the fancy new Houston Municipal Air Terminal that was just completed the year before. People had been using what is now William P. Hobby Airport since the late 1920s, although it was merely a 600-acre pasture with a wooden terminal. In 1937 the city bought the land and replaced the old terminal with a new facility that would provide a better experience for those prosperous enough to travel by air. The Art Deco–style 1940 terminal was designed by Austrian-born architect Joseph Finger, who also designed Houston's city hall. When the building was dedicated, the public was offered a tour of the facility; a lucky few won free local flights. Braniff Airways and Eastern Airlines were the only airlines that served the airport in its early years.

RIGHT: The 1940 terminal didn't see service for long, as air traffic from Houston increased quickly and outgrew the building. In 1954 the airport was renamed Houston International Airport, and the old terminal was leased as commercial and administrative space. It was renamed William P. Hobby Airport in 1967 after the state's twenty-seventh governor. By the late 1970s, some wanted to demolish the old terminal, but many preservationists couldn't bear the thought of seeing it felled by the wrecking ball, no matter how badly airport administrators wanted the extra space. It now serves as the Air Terminal Museum. Hobby Airport grew around the old terminal as it became a major regional airport. Southwest Airlines is a major part of the airport's traffic, running over 120 flights to thirty cities each day and taking up slots in seventeen of the airport's twenty-six gates. AirTran Airways, American Eagle, Delta Connection, and JetBlue Airways also service Hobby Airport.

BELOW: The Houston Municipal Air Terminal was one of many Houston commissions for architect Joseph Finger. He also designed the Texas State Hotel (1939), the Harris County Courthouse (1953), and the Barker Brothers Studio (1931), which is now the Lawndale Arts Center.

Municipal Airport, Houston, Texas

1962

NASA JOHNSON SPACE CENTER, HOUSTON
A giant leap for mankind

LEFT: This shot shows the control room at NASA's Johnson Space Center (JSC) in 1962. In 1961 President John F. Kennedy threw down the gauntlet to put a man on the moon by the end of the decade. But for this big goal, they needed a big space to work. The initiative's selection team chose Houston for its many technical workers, logistical infrastructure, mild climate, and proximity to both the San Jacinto Ordinance Depot and major academic institutions such as Rice University. Rice owned the land on which the JSC now stands, about twenty-five miles southeast of Houston near Galveston Bay. The university donated the undeveloped cattle-grazing land to NASA for the facility, which was originally called the Manned Spacecraft Center. It was renamed the Lyndon B. Johnson Space Center in 1973 to honor the late president. Fittingly, it was Texan Charles Duke who uttered the famous words from Mission Control in Houston after *Apollo 11*'s lunar module took longer than expected to reach the moon's surface: "Tranquility, we copy you on the ground. You got a bunch of guys about to turn blue. We're breathing again."

ABOVE: These days, the hardware is different—but the intensity is still the same. Over the years, the JSC served as primary flight control for NASA, supporting major space programs such as Gemini, Apollo, Skylab, the space shuttle, and the International Space Station. The JSC today is a complex campus of facilities, including what is now called the Christopher C. Kraft Jr. Mission Control Center, which has primary responsibility for coordinating and monitoring all manned American spaceflight. Its multiple rooms, computers, and controls used to handle those responsibilities look as if they come straight out of *Star Trek*. The site also houses extensive and elaborate training facilities, a moon rock lab, and the directors of the White Sands Test Facility in New Mexico. Building 30, the famous Apollo Mission Control Center, is now a National Historic Landmark.

1920

USS *TEXAS*

Together with the San Jacinto Monument, the old battleship and the old battle site are testaments to Texan valor

LEFT: This photo shows the battleship USS *Texas* (BB-35) in 1920. The *Texas* was christened in May 1912. Built in Newport News, Virginia, the *Texas* is a New York–class battleship that saw service in World War I and World War II. It was the first U.S. Navy battleship to use 14-inch, 45-caliber guns; it had ten of them. It was also armed with fifty-one 5-inch, 51-caliber guns and four submerged 21-inch torpedo tubes. The *Texas* served in the Atlantic Fleet during World War I. In World War II, the *Texas* served as the flagship for Allied landings at Omaha Beach on D-Day; it also supported landings in North Africa, southern France, Okinawa, and Iwo Jima. After three decades of service, the USS *Texas* became America's first memorial battleship and national park at the Battleship Texas State Historic Site.

LEFT: Old warriors never die; they just move on to another theater of battle. Today, the USS *Texas* faces the most relentless adversary of all: time. In 1983 the *Texas* fell under the aegis of the Texas Parks and Wildlife Department. Part of a vast parkland complex, it was restored to shipshape and spent decades as a museum. By 1988 it had been ravaged by rust and was towed to a Galveston shipyard for restoration; it was back in service in 1990. Millions have been spent on maintenance, repair, and restoration. A series of leaks in the 2000s plagued the ship's minders and generated a bit of negative press for the old warhorse. Fortunately, the Battleship Texas Foundation has taken the helm and is leading the *Texas* through a massive restoration, including a total replacement of the hull. The *Texas* has become a cherished landmark, an irreplaceable part of American naval history, and an icon of Texas fighting spirit.

35

ABOVE: The San Jacinto Monument and Museum, seen here on a 1940s postcard, commemorates the final battle of Texas independence from Mexican colonial rule, and those who fought for the cause. It was built between 1936 and 1939 (1936 marked 100 years since the battle was fought). Architect Alfred C. Finn designed the Art Deco–style monument, which was built by the Warren C. Bellows Construction Company. It is made of concrete faced with fossilized limestone quarried in central Texas. The monument stands at 570 feet tall, starting at a base that's 48 feet square and tapering to 30 feet square at the observation tower (topped by a 34-foot star). A 350,000-square-foot reflection pool complements the structure. Much has been made of the fact that it's taller than the Washington Monument. In fact, the two are the same size, measuring the San Jacinto from the first floor to the top. The base of the San Jacinto Monument is taller, however, making its total height 15 feet taller than the Washington Monument.

RIGHT: These days it's easy to lose the San Jacinto Monument amid a horizon of massive industrial development across Houston's east side in the city of La Porte. But up close, it's as grand as ever—and is now part of the San Jacinto Battleground State Historic Site. This 1,200-acre park offers both the monument and the battleship *Texas*, and the opportunity to explore the actual land on which the battle was fought. The grounds also have lots of wide-open marsh trails, coastal prairie, and bottomland forest for hiking and taking in some fresh coastal air. The museum comprising the base of the monument offers not just information but insight and inspiration. The view from the top of the monument and the thirty-five-minute *Texas Forever!* multimedia presentation are musts for visitors.

c.1940

MICHEL B. MENARD HOUSE, GALVESTON
The founder of Galveston built this grand house in 1838

LEFT: This shady, columned beauty from the Republic of Texas era belonged to a Quebecois who shrewdly traded in furs, real estate, and politics. Born in 1805, Michel B. Menard had made his way to Texas while it was still a Mexican colony. By dealing through brokers, he owned a respectable 40,000 acres by 1834. One of his deals included title to the then-vacant eastern end of Galveston Island—the owning of which was forbidden to non-Hispanics under Mexican colonial law. He sat on the claim until after the Texas Revolution, then swooped in with some partners and served as the founder of Galveston. His handsome Greek Revival–style home at 1605 Thirty-third Street is a treasure of residential architecture from the republic years. Like many wheeler-dealers, Menard's fortunes would ebb and flow—and they did more ebbing in his later years. Yet he retained the house until he passed away there in 1856.

ABOVE: If that's not an inviting porch, there's never been one. Today, the house is Galveston's oldest residential dwelling. Menard's relatives lived there until 1879, and then sold it to Edwin Ketchum—a poor, unfortunate soul who served as chief of police during the Great Storm of 1900. Ketchum's family owned the house until the 1970s. For a few decades after that, it seemed to be just another old house. By the 1990s, it was basically a flophouse, and the City of Galveston wanted to tear it down. Finally, it was purchased by someone who appreciated its historical value and meticulously restored it. The current owners have done a glorious job in bringing a piece of Texas history back from the grave, and today the house operates as both a museum and a popular venue of weddings, lectures, conferences, and parties. The Menard House is furnished in period furniture, and features a backyard gazebo perfect for ceremonies.

c.1970

TRUBE CASTLE, GALVESTON
A fairy-tale mansion dating to 1890

LEFT: The original owner of this distinctive 7,000-square-foot mansion on Sealy Avenue was wealthy merchant and real-estate magnate John C. Trube. Trube was Danish, and the house's whimsical Romantic Revival–style architecture was inspired by castles in Trube's homeland. It was built in just three months in 1890 for $9,700. Practically everything about the house, including its diagonal orientation on the property, is unusual and adventurous. Trube lived in Houston and, like many prominent Houstonians, dabbled in Galveston property. But he really made a statement with what would become known as the Trube Castle. This largess was representative of his family's style. He was one of three brothers in the area; all three brothers married daughters of the prominent Durst family. For almost a hundred years after its construction, a member of the Trube family lived in the mansion. In 1965 John's cousin Edwin bought the property, and was living there when this picture was taken.

c.1970

ABOVE: The Trube Castle still looks like it materialized from a dream. Time has only enhanced it, and the house makes even the handsome architecture of its stately neighbors seem modest. Edwin Trube's wife, Mary, was the last member of the family to reside there. She passed in 1985, leaving her property to charity. The Trube Castle eventually became a bed-and-breakfast. With thirty-three rooms to spare, it was well suited, but the enterprise didn't last,

and the house once again became a private residence, undergoing restorations, including a major overhaul in 1990—and a lot of ongoing maintenance. Practically every house in Galveston incurred some kind of damage during Hurricane Ike in 2008, and the castle was no exception. But its current owners have worked hard to keep this architectural gem looking good over the years, and it remains one of the most distinctive private residences in Texas.

LEFT: The building was designed by architect Alfred Muller, who combined Gothic style with the exuberance of the period, as the fashionable elite had mansions built in Galveston.

HOTEL GALVEZ, GALVESTON

After the disastrous hurricane of 1900, the hotel was a major boost to tourism

ABOVE: This photograph shows the grand Hotel Galvez in 1911, the year it opened. The onlookers on Seawall Boulevard could have been talking about the building's elaborate appointments, its Mission and Spanish Revival architecture, or the charming beach view. But what most people were talking about was the hotel's construction cost: a mind-blowing $1 million (equivalent to about $23 million today). For the island in 1911, it was worth the investment. For Texans and tourists, Galveston was the hottest thing since summer sand—consistently delivering a booming tourist trade. But the big storm in 1900 had put the brakes on island tourism. The seawall needed to be built higher and properties engineered better. The Galvez was a chance to get the party started again. It was named after Spanish statesman Bernardo de Gálvez—for whom the city is named. It soon earned the nickname "Queen of the Gulf," becoming the social hub of the island. A brochure passed out during its grand opening claimed it was "good enough for everybody and not too good for anybody."

BELOW: Aside from the cars and signs lining the street, the hotel's seawall entrance is essentially unchanged. Texas's only historic beachfront hotel, the Galvez has lasted an entire century and is still a popular destination for travelers who appreciate luxury with a historical patina. Of course, some years were better than others. During World War II, the U.S. Coast Guard occupied the hotel; one can only imagine the state of the bar. After the war, local gambling filled the hotel with movers and shakers (of martinis). Gambling was made illegal in the mid-1950s, and occupancy took a hit. The next few decades saw multiple ownership changes. Not every owner stuck to its original aesthetic. In 1995 oil magnate and Galveston native George P. Mitchell bought the Galvez and restored it. It's now a part of the Wyndham Hotels and Resorts franchise. Jimmy Stewart, Douglas MacArthur, Frank Sinatra, Howard Hughes, and several U.S. presidents have stayed at the Galvez.

LION DOLLAR
EL GALVEZ
WALL BOULEVARD
ESTON, TEXAS.

c.1911

GALVESTON STORM DAMAGE

The 1900 Storm Memorial commemorates the centennial of the Great Storm of 1900. Created in memory of the storm's victims, the 10-foot-tall bronze sculpture, titled *Place of Remembrance*, was created by Galveston native David Moore. A nearby plaque tells the story of the storm. During the monument's dedication in 2000, the names of storm victims were placed in a vault beneath the sculpture. Rose petals were also scattered in the water from a U.S. Coast Guard vessel. The memorial is at Forty-eighth Street and Seawall Boulevard.

85

c.1970

BISHOP'S PALACE, GALVESTON
Shelter to many during the devastating hurricane of 1900

c.1970

ABOVE: The American Institute of Architects has listed the Bishop's Palace (Gresham's Castle) as one of the 100 most significant buildings in the United States.

LEFT: The view from Broadway and Fourteenth Street accentuates the distinctive Victorian architecture of this structure that, even in its day, was striking. Located at 1402 Broadway, the house was built for railroad tycoon and politician Walter Gresham. Gresham was the Galveston district attorney for a time, as well as a congressman. Gresham had nine children, so the home was built to last. Construction started in 1887 and was finished in 1892. It was designed by local architect Nicholas Clayton. The closer one looks at the house, inside or out, the more it has to offer. The builder used stones of different colors and shapes, as well as steel, for the house's exterior—a decision that would pay off later. Inside, it sports Sienna marble columns, stained glass practically everywhere, a massive mahogany fireplace, and tall, beautifully plastered ceilings.

RIGHT: Today, its landscaping and careful maintenance honor the house's beauty. Walter Gresham died in 1920. When his wife Josephine sold the place in 1923, it was to the Catholic Diocese of Galveston, to be used as a residence for the bishop (hence the name). By then it had proven itself not just a distinctive architectural gem but also one of the safest places to live on the island. Its design and materials helped it survive the devastating storm of 1900 almost unscathed. Supposedly, Josephine Gresham lashed herself to the porch and pulled people out of the water as the storm surge raced through the streets. The bishop lived there until his death in 1950. During his tenure, he turned one of the rooms into a chapel. Today, it's in what is now Galveston's East End Historic District and is listed in the National Register of Historic Places. The Galveston Historical Foundation offers guided tours of the house seven days a week.

1936

U.S. CUSTOM HOUSE, GALVESTON

Predating the Civil War, this building has survived everything that nature and Yankee cannons have thrown at it

LEFT: The old U.S. Custom House as it stood in the summer of 1936. The building served as a federal courthouse. Wherever you find commerce, you'll find taxes—so it's no surprise that the U.S. Customs Service is the nation's oldest federal agency. This elegant building was originally built in 1861 just as the Civil War erupted. It was completed in just 114 days, a pace of construction that was unheard of in those days. Galveston was a logistically critical port for Confederate and Union forces, and the building saw much traffic as shipping, ideology, and cannon fire crisscrossed the island. It escaped the war unscathed, and likewise avoided damage from Galveston's terrible fire of 1885. In 1917 a courtroom was built on the second floor and it began its judicial duty on behalf of Washington, D.C.

ABOVE: The building drew a number of occupants over the years, many federally oriented (including a post office). After a hundred years of service, it was looking worse for the wear. James Noel and his family stepped in to lead a major restoration effort, which was completed in 1967 to much fanfare. A formal rededication of the building was held, and the U.S. Postal Service even issued a stamp depicting the building. But as much as people loved it, it didn't attract many private-sector tenants. The building was added to the National Register of Historic Places in 1970, but within a few years it was nearly empty. Today, it serves as the headquarters for the Galveston Historical Foundation (GHF). The GHF is Texas's oldest (and the nation's second-oldest) historical preservation group. Serving as a steward, advocate, and educator on behalf of Galveston's iconic historical properties, the GHF uses the building as a public research and exhibition center.

c.1965

GALVESTON STRAND HISTORIC DISTRICT

Saved from progress and redevelopment by Houston's booming port business

c.1965

ABOVE: The Kaufman and Runge Building at 222 Twenty-second Street and Avenue C.

LEFT: The First National Bank Building at 2127 Avenue B (the Strand).

LEFT: The buildings making up what we now call the Strand today in Galveston date back to the mid-nineteenth century. "The Strand" is actually Avenue B. The nickname for this area is attributed to a German immigrant named Michael Shaw, who owned a jewelry store at Twenty-third Street and Avenue B. He didn't think that "Avenue B" had a very posh ring to it, so he started calling it "the Strand" after the famous road in London. Somehow the name stuck. Galveston's port was the busiest in the area at the time, shuffling nearly a thousand ships in and out each day. The old Victorian-style shops along the Strand did a brisk business. Despite damage inflicted to many of the area's buildings in the Civil War, it's estimated that in 1881 shops on the Strand did around $38 million worth of business. After the Great Storm of 1900, many Strand buildings were damaged and the area became a more nondescript warehouse district.

ABOVE: In the 1900s, Houston came out of nowhere as a port city by constructing an artificial deepwater shipping channel. As a result, many of Galveston's seaport businesses left. On the upside, that meant many of the Strand's old historic buildings were not demolished in the name of economic progress. Preservationists stepped in to restore select buildings on the Strand in the 1960s and 1970s. The Strand Historic District was declared a National Historic Landmark District in 1976. Dozens of historically significant buildings, both big and small, make up about twenty-six blocks of businesses paralleling Harborside Drive. Some of the more notable include Hendley Row (1859), the J. S. Brown Hardware Company Building (1870), the Rosenburg Building (1870s), and the W. L. Moody Building (1884). Several companies offer guided tours through the area. The first weekend in December, the Strand celebrates the holidays with Dickens on the Strand—a Christmas parade and celebration where people dress in Victorian period costumes.

c.1905

BEAUMONT OIL EXCHANGE

The rush to extract oil coincided with a rush to make money from bogus oil companies

ABOVE: Around 600 oil companies were formed when the oil boom at Spindletop took off. Some companies were more scrupulous than others. So many investors lost money on bogus oil wells around the area that it was nicknamed "Swindletop." In response, the Beaumont Oil Exchange and Board of Trade was incorporated on April 18, 1901 (just four months after the big

"Lucas Gusher" hit). The stock exchange in New York was a long way off—and the oil business needed something on the ground that could keep pace. The exchange's charter was to set standards, processes, and protocols to help protect the interests of investors. The company consolidated with a similar concern in 1903 to become the Beaumont Oil Exchange and Board of Trade.

c.1905

ABOVE: A forest of derricks at the Spindletop oil field.

RIGHT: The exchange was eventually dissolved, along with most of Gladys City, which surrounded the original Spindletop. The original exchange is long gone. But this replica built at the Gladys City–Spindletop Boomtown Museum gives visitors a taste of the old makeshift trading floor. With so many people tapping into the reservoir, the area's production fell off of a cliff. When the oil exchange hit its heyday in 1902, the field's production was 17.5 million barrels per day. By February 1904, it had dwindled to just 10,000 per day. A lot less oil meant a lot fewer oil companies. Most of those original companies listed on the exchange simply dried up and blew away. Those who didn't went on to continue production in other oil fields, consolidating and doubling down over the years to eventually become the companies we know today, such as Texaco, Mobil, Gulf (now Chevron) and Humble (later Exxon). Those companies would eventually migrate to other financial exchanges.

1901

SPINDLETOP, BEAUMONT

Texas was a cotton and cattle state until Anthony Lucas started drilling near Beaumont

ABOVE: The Spindletop oil field changed the Texas economic landscape forever, transforming it into the world's energy capital almost overnight. Drilling on a salt dome formation near Beaumont, Anthony Lucas struck it rich on land he had leased from the Gladys City Company. He drilled there for a few years without success, but his day would come. The Lucas Gusher, which is the derrick shown here, came in on January 10, 1901. This picture was taken that same year. The well blew a 100-foot fountain of black gold for nine days until it could be capped for production (at 100,000 barrels per day). It was an unprecedented amount of production; Beaumont grew fivefold and land prices skyrocketed. One well, drilled for $10,000 prior to the activation of the Lucas Gusher, was sold for $1.25 million. Hordes of people became millionaires overnight. Agriculture and shipping no longer controlled the state's economy; oil was king.

94

1901

ABOVE: Storage for the Star and Crescent Oil Company. It was thriving in 1901, but by 1902 it was bankrupt and the assets were bought by the Sun Oil Company, which would eventually become part of Sunoco.

RIGHT: Spindletop declined quickly, but sparked a flood of wildcatters statewide who transformed the state's industrial, technical, and economic progress. In 1941 the pink granite marker seen on the left was erected near the Lucas Gusher site. Eventually, the developments surrounding the Spindletop field dwindled and died as the reservoir fizzled out over the years. Buildings were demolished, and land was sold for other purposes. The granite monument was moved to a re-creation of Spindletop's boom times at the Spindletop–Gladys City Boomtown Museum (the museum's replica of the Lucas Gusher can be seen on the right). Located on the campus of Beaumont's Lamar University, the museum allows visitors to experience boomtown life. Many of the exhibits use actual period equipment from the boomtown days. The museum and its replicas are run by the university.

1936

ANSON JONES HOUSE, WASHINGTON-ON-THE-BRAZOS
While his estate thrived, the political career of the fourth president of Texas hit the buffers

LEFT: This shot shows the Washington-on-the-Brazos home of Texas's last president, Anson Jones, in 1936—a hundred years after Texas declared its independence from Mexico. Jones moved to Texas in 1833, where his medical practice thrived and he became politically active in the Texas patriot movement. Jones was a Freemason, and during the Texas Revolution he served as a surgeon and judge advocate. The house was built for him in 1844, the year he was elected president of the Republic of Texas. While many leaders of the republic were banking on rapid annexation into the United States, Jones held his ground on several issues hoping for—if not the best terms possible for the people of Texas—true long-term Texas independence. He lived here until his untimely death in 1858. It was a part of his family's plantation, which was named Barrington in honor of his Massachusetts birthplace. On this land, the Jones family grew cotton and corn, and raised cattle and hogs.

RIGHT: After Texas's annexation into the union, Jones faded into the political background, but his plantation thrived. In 1936, the centennial of the Republic of Texas, the Anson Jones House became part of the Washington-on-the-Brazos State Historic Site. Texas Parks and Wildlife bought the site in 1976, and today it is once again a working plantation and state park. Visitors to Barrington Living Farm can experience life on an old Texas plantation just as it was in the republic days. Visitors can feed the chickens and help plant crops. Jones's original zeal for Texas independence is also once again up and running. A surprisingly large number of Texans support secession from the United States, based mostly on grounds of preserving Texans' civil liberties and economic responsibility. In 2013 the White House received numerous "Texas secession" petition signatures from citizens and heated rhetoric from the Texas governor to prompt a formal response from the U.S. government. Unsurprisingly, the response was no.

LEFT: The inside of the Anson Jones House is stacked with period antiques and replicas depicting life at the time when the Jones family occupied the house. In the farmhouse, Mr. and Mrs. Jones shared their room with their two youngest children. The house is built of pine, cedar, and oak. After annexation, Jones never got over the fact that his predecessor, Sam Houston, and Thomas Jefferson Rusk were chosen over him to represent Texas in the senate. He shot himself in Houston's Old Capitol Hotel in 1858.

c.1930

TEXAS A&M UNIVERSITY, COLLEGE STATION

Offering classes in agriculture and mechanic arts since 1876

ABOVE: Texas A&M University's College Station campus as viewed from the West Gate entrance around 1930. In 1866 the decision was made to create a Texas university based on lands provided in the 1862 Morrill Act. The Texas legislature officially established the school in 1871 to provide higher learning for the study of science, the classics, military tactics, and "agriculture and mechanic arts." Classes started in 1876, and students were soon known as "Aggies." The stone pillar in the center of the road is the West Gate Memorial, commemorating Aggies who gave their lives fighting in World War I. The year 1930 was notable in Texas A&M tradition, as it was the year that first saw the "Gig 'em, Aggies!" thumbs-up symbol emerge as a result of yell practice before a football game (the term "gig" is used when frog hunting). College Station was designated a city in its own right in 1938.

ABOVE: The Texas A&M marching band photographed in 1902.

ABOVE: The main entrance changed in 1932 from the west, facing the railroad, to the east, facing Highway 6. The Systems Administration Building became the new grand entrance building.

BELOW: Today one of the state's leading universities, the campus would be barely recognizable to an early graduate. However, the principles and values of the institution are the same. Texas A&M is not only an institution of higher learning but also a Texas cultural institution. Aggies take honor and tradition seriously. The West Gate Memorial shown in the archival photo was moved to the corner of Simpson Drill Field upon construction of the Albritton Tower on campus, which was donated in 1984. Texas A&M now has over 50,000 students, and the campus is like a city in itself. Some of the most popular attractions include the George Bush Presidential Library and Museum, and the Kyle Field football stadium. Along with the Citadel and the Virginia Military Institute, Texas A&M is one of just six "senior military" colleges to offer Reserve Officers Training Corps (ROTC) programs in the United States.

1910

BAYLOR UNIVERSITY, WACO
The second site of the university, formerly located at Independence

ABOVE: This panoramic view of the Baylor campus was taken in 1910. The shot shows, left to right, the F. L. Carroll Chapel, Georgia Burleson Hall, the Old Main Building, and the George W. Carroll Science Hall. These four buildings form what's known as the Rufus C. Burleson Quadrangle—the heart of Baylor. The Old Main Building (1887) was at one point the school's only classroom building. That's a statue of the school's first president, Dr. Rufus C. Burleson, in the center. Known today as a Waco institution, this is not the first Baylor campus. Its original campus was actually in Independence, Texas. The Independence campus was split between two hills—men on one, women on the other. A stream separated them, referred to by students as the "River Jordan" because on the other side was the "Promised Land." In 1885 the men moved to Baylor to form this campus. The women moved to nearby Belton, Texas, to form the Baylor Female College (now the University of Mary Hardin-Baylor).

RIGHT: The quadrangle and its original four buildings look much the same today—though it was a close call. The library and chapel were gutted by fire in 1922. The building was rebuilt and is today still a functioning library (chapel services are held elsewhere). Burleson Hall is now an administrative building. There is a lot more campus, because there are a lot more students these days. Baylor University has now grown to an enrollment of over 15,000 students who come from every state in United States, as well as seventy-three countries. In 1996 the school repealed its 150-year ban on dancing—and the grassy lawns shown here at the quadrangle were covered with dancers enjoying the seventeen-piece Haskett-Burleson Band. One of the lead members of the band, Ed Burleson, was Rufus C. Burleson's great-grandson.

c.1940

WACO SUSPENSION BRIDGE
Commerce boomed when the bridge replaced the ferry

RIGHT: This shot of the original suspension bridge crossing the Brazos River in downtown Waco was taken in the 1870s. It officially opened in 1870; it was Texas's first major suspension bridge, and the only bridge crossing the Brazos. Before then, those who wanted to cross the river took a ferry. The distinctive brick structure was composed of approximately three million bricks, all fired in Waco. But everything else had to be ferried from Galveston to Bryan—and then hauled in by oxen. The cables from the bridge were made in Trenton, New Jersey. Though it cost $141,000 to build, it had a monopoly on traffic crossing the Brazos and charged a nickel per head. It was quite the luxury, as its width meant room for cattle and people and cargo all at once. With Waco's proximity to the Chisholm Trail, the bridge was an instant success. The above photo shows the bridge in the 1940s.

c.1870

ABOVE: The bridge helped Waco develop into a commercial hub. In 1914 it saw a major overhaul with new cables and trusses, increasing the bridge's load capacity. The automobile began comprising most of the bridge's traffic. With over a century of service, and monstrous American sedans and eighteen-wheelers now crossing, the state decided to give the bridge a break. It was marked for foot traffic only in 1971, with a newer, more modern bridge built next to it for vehicular traffic. Now listed on the National Register of Historic Places, the Waco Suspension Bridge today connects two parks on either side. It's a popular spot to catch fireworks on the Fourth of July, and is frequented by runners and walkers looking for a safe and scenic spot to do a workout. The two buildings in the background are the Hilton Waco and the old ALICO Building built in 1910—the city's tallest building.

1939

SOUTH SECOND STREET, WACO
Downtown Waco was transformed in a generation

ABOVE: These gentlemen are catching up on the day's events down at the Brazos Fish Market in Waco's Market Square in 1939. Waco at that time was largely an agricultural center that woke up with the chickens and wasn't afraid to get its hands dirty. Of course, a few of these guys might have been working hard at finding a job, too. The Great Depression and the 1930s in general weren't kind to Waco. Farmers had to cut back spending, and businesses were laying off employees. New Deal programs and the Works Progress Administration were pumping taxpayer money into the city through federal programs, but true organic economic recovery wouldn't come until World War II. The Brazos Fish Market at 114 South Second Street looked like it was still doing fine, however. This picture was taken as part of a government project to document the ravages of the Great Depression nationwide.

ABOVE: The Brazos Fish Market, along with much of downtown Waco, was destroyed during the tornado of 1953. Several Market Square buildings were destroyed as well as many of the blocks surrounding the area. Bridge Street and the businesses there were completely obliterated—literally wiped off the map (today Bridge Street only exists on the east side of the river, not by downtown). In the book *Texas Storms: Tales of Raging Weather in the Lone Star State*, Waco resident Emanuel Rubel reports having been in the Brazos Fish Market during the twister. After seeing a blue car flipping down Second Street end over end, he took shelter inside a two-foot-square butcher's block—which protected him from the building when it collapsed down around him. The Market Square and Bridge Street area was never rebuilt as it was, and today the Waco Convention Center and miscellaneous parking lots cover the area where the old fishmongers once sold catfish, carp, and bass fillets.

c.1960

TEXAS COUNTY COURTHOUSES

Hill County is regarded as one of the best little courthouses in Texas

ABOVE: The Hill County Courthouse in Hillsboro was completed in 1890. Designed by W. C. Dodson, a prominent Waco architect who designed several Texas courthouses, it sports a distinctive blend of Second Empire and Italianate architecture. The building, made of Bell County limestone, is three stories high, but its tower stood at seven stories with a clock. The tower also housed a 1,525-pound bell cast at the McShane Bell Foundry (which is still in business). Even high-tone East Coast media chimed in on its beauty. *Harper's* magazine called it "an outstanding cathedral." This building was actually the fourth courthouse to serve the county, replacing a plain brick predecessor that was built in 1874. Brownsville contractors Lovell, Miller & Hood built the courthouse for a grand total of $83,000. Both Hillsboro and Hill County were named for Dr. George W. Hill, who was secretary of war for the Republic of Texas.

c.1945

ABOVE: On New Year's Day 1993, tragedy struck the courthouse. A fire caused by an electrical short ripped through the structure. Its sturdy limestone walls were undamaged, but the third floor and clock tower were done for. The massive bell crashed through to the second-floor courtroom while firefighters from more than fifteen companies worked overtime to save what they could. When the embers cooled from the gutted building, there wasn't an insurance firm around that wouldn't have mandated the wrecking ball. What saved it? People loved this old courthouse. The architects hired to restore the courthouse, ArchiTexas of Dallas, had to use their imagination in re-creating it, as no actual blueprints existed. They used the courthouse at Granbury as a template—and interviewed people who used to work there before the fire. Several parties donated funds, including Hill County native Willie Nelson. The restoration was completed in 1999 and, as can be seen here, the courthouse looks as good as old.

ABOVE RIGHT: The Parker County Courthouse in Weatherford (just west of Fort Worth) is another one of W. C. Dodson's architectural masterpieces. At the time, he was working with a partner named W. W. Dudley. The three-story, Second Empire building has a fourth-story attic and a tall clock tower that much resembles the Dodson design of the Hill County Courthouse. This was the fourth Parker County Courthouse, and was completed in 1886. The building cost $55,555.55 and is made of native Texas limestone. The facade is split up into five tall units. One interesting aspect of the building's design is how the second- and third-story windows span both floors. Its distinctive convex mansard roof dominated the landscape in its day.

RIGHT: At one point, the big district courtroom was divided into offices. In 2004 the courthouse's interior saw a major renovation. Among the work was restoring the courtroom to its original size, re-creating the elaborate wall and ceiling paintings, replacing the patterned flooring and small wood balconies—as well as taking care of basics such as new plumbing and electrical work.

c.1925

OLD RED COURTHOUSE, DALLAS
The grand Romanesque building presiding over Dealey Plaza

LEFT: The Old Red Courthouse at 100 South Houston Street, a distinctive Romanesque Revival building, was the fifth courthouse to serve on this land (all its predecessors burned). At the time of the building's construction, Dallas County was mostly rural. By the time the building was completed in 1882, Dallas County's population had surged following the Civil War. Southerners from across the Confederacy flocked to Dallas for fertile farmland. The courthouse was a response to this growth. The building's architect was German-born Max Orlopp Jr. It was built of red sandstone and granite, to make it as fireproof as possible given the fate of its predecessors. The building originally had a clock tower with a three-ton bell. It was so loud, however, it threatened to shake the building apart, and so it was removed in 1919. The cabin in front is the restored John Neely Bryan Cabin, an early home of the city's founder and its first "courthouse."

RIGHT: By 1966 Dallas County had outgrown the building and the courts were moved to a more modern building nearby. This was a period of rapid growth; the number of employees in every major Dallas County industry tripled between 1953 and 1989. "Old Red" was added to the National Register of Historic Places in 1976, but it had seen better days. In 2001 an initiative to restore the building was undertaken. Around $23 million was generated to restore the building to its original appearance and condition—and transform it into a museum celebrating the area's history. Local architect James Pratt oversaw the building's restoration, which included a replica of the building's old clock tower. Pratt is the Indiana Jones of Dallas architecture; unable to locate the building's original plans, he relied on old photographs and hands-on exploration of the structure. Datum Engineers of Dallas and Thos. S. Byrne of Fort Worth supported the restoration as the project's structural engineer and contractor, respectively.

DEALEY PLAZA, DALLAS
Inextricably linked to the assassination of JFK

BELOW: The 1930s were a time of rapid modernization, and city planning was no exception. Dallas residents beamed with pride when, in 1935, the city created a triple freeway underpass. To help manage traffic on the western edge of downtown Dallas, what the *Dallas Morning News* called "the front door of Dallas," three major streets—Elm, Main, and Commerce—were sloped down into one. The road ducked under a railroad bridge designed in the Art Deco style. The resulting space was named after the project's champion, *Dallas*

Morning News publisher George Bannerman Dealey. But by the time this picture was taken, this modest green space had already become infamous as the site of the 1963 assassination of John F. Kennedy, the thirty-fifth president of the United States. This scene shows the U.S. Secret Service re-creating the scene of Kennedy's assassination for investigative purposes. Flowers for the fallen president, as well as a number of spectators, dotted the plaza that day.

1963

BELOW: Visitors continue to pay their respects to the fallen president (the Old Red Courthouse is seen on the left). The flowers on the plaza never stopped, and decades later the area became an unofficial memorial to President Kennedy. In 1970 the John F. Kennedy Memorial Plaza—a cenotaph designed by architect Philip Johnson—was dedicated one block east of Dealey Plaza between Main and Commerce Streets. In 1993 Dealey Plaza was officially recognized as a National Historic Landmark District. On the sixth and seventh floors of what was once known as the Texas School Book Depository (the building from which Kennedy was shot) now stands the Sixth Floor Museum at Dealey Plaza. A somber and enriching experience, the museum's permanent exhibit on the sixth floor features media and artifacts chronicling the life and legacy of John F. Kennedy. The seventh floor offers monthly programs, and its impressive reading room is open to the public.

ABOVE: The view from the Texas School Book Depository window looking down on Dealey Plaza. Oliver Stone's movie *JFK* glossed over the fact that assassin Lee Harvey Oswald had been graded between "sharpshooter" and "marksman" during his time with the U.S. Marines.

1912

ADOLPHUS HOTEL, DALLAS
Still one of the swankiest hotels in Texas

LEFT: Workers are clearing the land at 1315 Commerce Street for the Adolphus Hotel in 1912. The hotel was being built by Anheuser-Busch founder Adolphus Busch (from which it obviously took its name). Busch bought the land from the City of Dallas, and hired the architectural firm of Barnett, Hayes, and Barnett out of St. Louis (who also designed Busch's mausoleum). The building was constructed from red brick and gray granite, with a slate and bronze mansard roof. It stood at twenty-one stories—the tallest building in Texas at the time. Among the hotel's intricate design features was a Budweiser beer-shaped turret in one corner of the building. The hotel opened its doors in 1915, and quickly became an icon of Texas's oil-boom prosperity.

BELOW: A postcard of the Adolphus from the 1920s showing the hotel complete with the "Bud" tower.

THE ADOLPHUS HOTEL, DALLAS.

ABOVE: In the years since its christening, the Adolphus has undergone a number of additions from various architects. In 1981 it saw a major restoration and remodeling—but over the decades this grand old establishment never lost its luster. The Adolphus today still carries the same level of mystique and majesty it did before the days when Dallas was a city of skyscrapers and franchise luxury hotels. Its sumptuously appointed spaces are still not quite rivaled by much of anything on the continent. Guests at the hotel over the years have included Queen Elizabeth II, the Vanderbilt family, U2, Babe Ruth, and several American presidents. Busch's brewery is today part of AB InBev, the world's largest brewery. The occasional ghost story makes the place even more alluring—such as the supposed sighting of a deceased customer of the hotel's bistro allegedly seen at her usual table.

c.1955

DALLAS HALL
The building at the core of Southern Methodist University

ABOVE: These sporty ladies are posing in front of Southern Methodist University's Dallas Hall in the mid-1950s. The building was the first on campus; the cornerstone was laid on November 28, 1912, to considerable fanfare. The university was founded by the United Methodist Church; its classes started on campus in 1915. Dallas Hall got its name in appreciation for the people of Dallas, who supported the school financially and politically upon its founding. Designed by the architectural firm of Shepley, Rutan, and Collidge, the building was inspired by both the Roman Pantheon and the library that Thomas Jefferson designed at the University of Virginia in Charlottesville. The building's dome is made of copper, with a rotunda topped with a brilliant stained-glass oculus. At the time, it housed the entirety of the school's classes, as well as its offices, piano practice rooms, a post office, and even a hamburger grill.

114

ABOVE: The campus has grown, but Dallas Hall is still where all the action is at SMU. In 1970 the building underwent a $1.9 million renovation that included classroom upgrades, an auditorium, an elevator, and a number of aesthetic enhancements, including the addition of the school seal on the rotunda floor. The seal is held as sacrosanct, rumor being that any student who steps on the seal won't graduate. Each student at SMU starts off with a tradition known as the "Rotunda Passage," whereby newbies are marched through Dallas Hall, out onto the quad, and into McFarlin Auditorium to begin their harried life at the university. Today SMU is considered a great place not only to learn but make heavy-hitting social connections. With an enrollment of just over 6,000 students, it's still an intimate and exclusive school that's built a loyal following in both the local and Methodist communities.

c.1910

TEXAS STATE FAIRGROUNDS, DALLAS

Home to the larger-than-life Big Tex, who has welcomed millions to the state fair

ABOVE: The Texas State Fair was incorporated in 1886 by a group of Dallas businessmen. In 1904, after a fire at the facility, the enterprise was taking huge financial losses on the ground's operation. So the City of Dallas purchased the eighty-acre site in East Dallas that came to be known as Fair Park. In the early 1900s, a full-on auto show was started. And while that might seem like pretty tame entertainment, the 1936 Texas Centennial Exposition held at Fair Park drew more than six million people. Celebrating a hundred years of Texas independence, the grand affair was planned years in advance and involved an act of Congress. Dallas was chosen as the site, because it paid for the privilege. Congress appropriated $3 million and Dallas kicked in over $7 million. In the end, the total spent on the exposition was $250 million. It occupied fifty buildings, some of which are still in use at Fair Park. Visitors to the Centennial Exposition experienced all kinds of things, including the "Cavalcade of Texas" historical exhibit, replica dinosaurs, and a car rigged to be driven by a saddle-mounted cowboy riding the hood.

ABOVE: Today's fairgrounds look more modern, and have expanded to 277 acres. The Cotton Bowl football stadium was added in 1930, and in the 1950s Big Tex (left) arrived—a fifty-two-foot-tall cowboy who greets fairgoers. An electrical fire burned Big Tex in 2012, but he was too much a part of the show to be scrapped. Livestock is still a big part of the show. And the auto show lives on, with a 300,000-square-foot exhibition space and outdoor truck area. New cars are on display, along with the "Classic Corral," where vintage car collectors showcase their projects. Live music abounds, and old-time competitions that showcase baking, needlepoint, and other skills are still popular. And it just wouldn't be a state fair if it didn't offer corn dogs and a wild assortment of other fried foods, as well as classic Texas barbecue. You can see the fair in action from the last Friday in September and throughout the following twenty-four days.

1932

TEXAS THEATRE, DALLAS

The first movie house in town with full air-conditioning

LEFT: The Texas Theatre opened in 1931. A group of five businessmen, spearheaded by Oak Cliff entrepreneur C. R. "Uncle Mack" McHenry, spared no expense in making this theater the grandest movie house in Texas. At 231 West Jefferson Boulevard in Oak Cliff, it was the place to see and be seen. It is best known as the place where Lee Harvey Oswald was arrested. But before that, it was known for one thing above all else: air-conditioning. It was the first Dallas theater with such a system, and for just a nickel, hot and bothered Texans could spend an afternoon luxuriating in the cool air. The water-cooled chiller used a 4,000-gallon tank to blow 200,000 cubic feet of air per minute across grateful patrons looking to escape the brutal Texas heat. That night's movie, 1932's *Red Dust*, wasn't helping the heat. A steamy romance, it was made prior to Hollywood's era of heavy censorship.

RIGHT: Today, Dallas feels just as hot as it did in the 1930s—and the Texas Theatre is a whole other kind of cool. The theater is still bringing big-screen glitz to the Big D even after all these years, via classic and foreign films, art-house flicks, retro kitsch, private screenings, and other features. It's also a popular venue for special events, with a cool bar. Aviation Cinemas owns the theater, but before they came onto the scene, its story was more *Grapes of Wrath* than *The Great Gatsby*. The theater was owned by United Artists when it was closed the first time in 1989. After that, a series of well-meaning groups repeatedly raised funds that just staved off the wrecking ball. Finally, Aviation took over in 2010. Today, its troubled financial past seems miles away. The theater buzzes with the ebb and flow of filmmakers, history lovers, movie geeks, hipsters, businesspeople, and those who just want to chill.

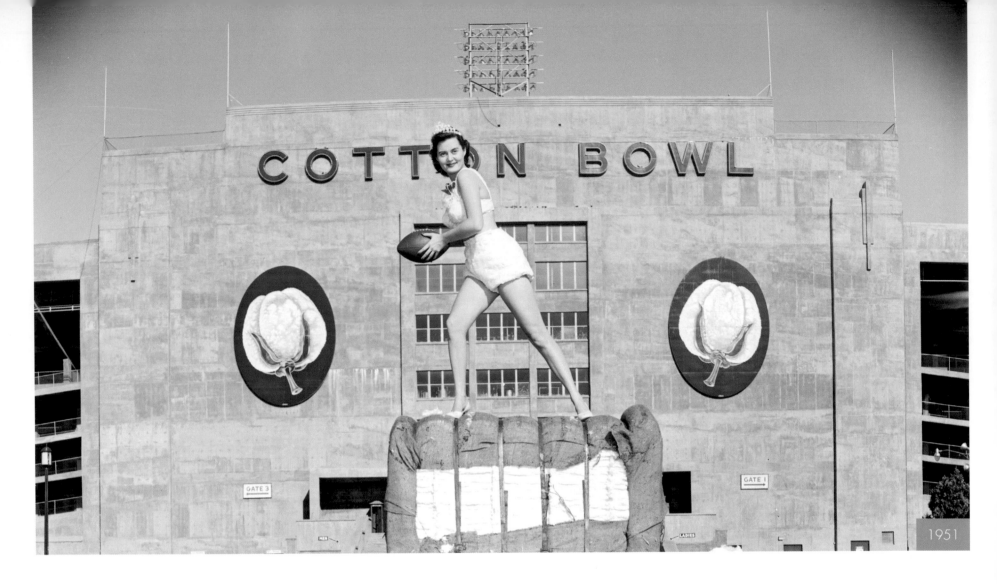

1951

COTTON BOWL, DALLAS

The stadium in Fair Park may have lost the fixture, but it still hosts big college games

ABOVE: This photo was taken in 1951, with local beauty JoAnne Hill atop an iconic cotton bale. The Cotton Bowl is the second stadium here at Fair Park. The first stadium was a 15,000-seat affair built for a local prizefight. Ground broke in 1930 for this facility, which had a 46,000-seat capacity. It was originally called the Fair Park Bowl, but the name was changed in 1936 when the stadium hosted the first Cotton Bowl Classic. The Cotton Bowl Classic was a college football bowl game that matched the winner of the Southwest Conference against another top-ranked

team. The first Cotton Bowl Classic in the stadium pitted Texas Christian University against Marquette University. TCU won that game 16–6 in front of a crowd of 17,000. In the 1951 Cotton Bowl Classic, in the year this picture was taken, the University of Tennessee staged an exciting fourth-quarter rally to defeat the University of Texas 20–14.

RIGHT: The addition of two upper decks in the late 1940s raised the capacity to 75,504.

1954

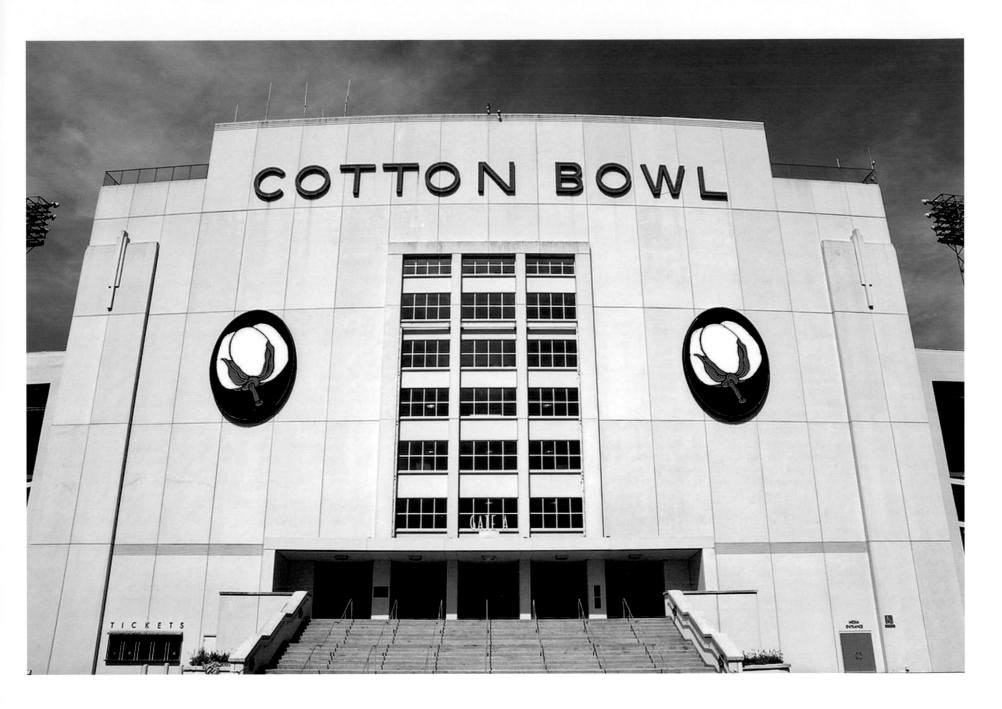

ABOVE: Today, the city works hard at keeping the Cotton Bowl in shape. It's become a local institution, necessitating expansions. The Dallas Cowboys called the stadium home from 1960 until 1971. But its use as a venue for college football has been legendary. By 1992 the Cotton Bowl was *the* game to attend—with a television audience of 20 million avid fans. In 1997 the Southwest Conference was dissolved, but the Cotton Bowl Classic lives on, pairing top teams from other conferences. The game proved more popular than the venue. In 2007 the game's organizers moved the Cotton Bowl Classic from the actual Cotton Bowl to Cowboys Stadium.

The Cotton Bowl is also the venue for the annual Red River Shootout—a rivalry between the University of Texas and the University of Oklahoma.

TURNPIKE STADIUM / RANGERS BALLPARK
Arlington Stadium heralded the arrival of Major League Baseball to Dallas

ABOVE: Turnpike Stadium was transformed into Arlington Stadium with the arrival of the Texas Rangers—formerly the Washington Senators. It was originally home to the Fort Worth Cats, who became the Dallas–Fort Worth Spurs.

c.1975

FAR LEFT: Minor league baseball was once a major deal in the Metroplex. What was eventually known as Arlington Stadium was originally Turnpike Stadium, built for Dallas–Fort Worth minor league teams. It broke ground in 1964, and when the facility opened in 1965 it was a fine place to spend a warm spring night in Texas. The circular field originally housed 10,000 fans. Then in 1972, the major league Washington Senators franchise relocated to the Dallas–Fort Worth area and was rebranded the Texas Rangers. To host them, Turnpike Stadium was renamed Arlington Stadium and underwent a number of expansions to eventually accommodate just over 40,000 fans. Especially popular with the locals were designated "Bat Night" games, where children under the age of twelve received a free baseball bat that they could bang on the stadium's metal bleachers. High summer temperatures in the area led to the majority of the Rangers' games being played at night.

BELOW: Over time, the Texas Rangers grew more popular. As the facility aged, the city lamented its limited capacity to house fans (and generate revenue). In 1994 Arlington Stadium was demolished to make way for Rangers Ballpark in Arlington—a quarter-mile away from the old stadium site. The photograph below shows the homes of two major Texas sports franchises side by side: Rangers Ballpark on the left and Cowboys Stadium on the right. But Rangers Ballpark isn't just a ballpark. The new stadium sits on a 270-acre complex housing an office building, numerous clubs and restaurants, a youth baseball park, a twelve-acre lake and public park space, fifteen parking lots, and a 1,200-speaker sound system. The total cost for the site was around $191 million. While that's a long way from a shared-use minor league park, the Dallas–Fort Worth area has changed since the old stadium was built. The population of the Rangers Ballpark area as a whole has grown to over six million people.

c.1910

CARNEGIE PUBLIC LIBRARY OF FORT WORTH

It started with just 7,000 books

ABOVE: Fort Worth's library traces its origin to the Fort Worth Public Library Association, a group of women who met at the home of Jenny Scheuber in 1892. Their mission was to get Fort Worth a public library worthy of the growing metropolis. The group got a state charter and a lot of momentum, but there was only one man to see about the topic of funding libraries at the time: Andrew Carnegie. The Scottish-American steel magnate spent his latter years as a philanthropist and donated funds for the construction of over 2,500 libraries worldwide. He advised Scheuber and her colleagues to raise money by asking the men of Fort Worth to contribute merely "the cost of a good cigar" toward the effort. The ladies went to work. After the city council approved $4,000 per year to support the library moving forward, Carnegie himself kicked in $50,000 of his own money. The Fort Worth Library opened in 1901.

ABOVE: The fine building Carnegie helped fund at Ninth and Throckmorton Streets didn't last long, but it made an impression. At first, it was just the librarian and five staffers (plus 7,000 books). It also sported its own art gallery. Soon the library turned up its service, delivering books around town and then branching out with another library building on the north side in 1921. By the late 1920s, the old building was bursting at the seams. In 1938 the Carnegie Library was razed, and in 1939 the city dedicated a new central library building (seen to the right) that was over four times the size of the Carnegie Library (the original granite cornerstone commemorates the old structure). With a bigger facility, the library then grew apace with the city. It started a bookmobile service in 1948, making twenty-eight stops around town. Branches were opened all across the area; today, the Fort Worth Library has sixteen branches in the area.

c.1940

FORT WORTH STOCKYARDS
The economic engine behind Fort Worth in the 1940s

ABOVE: The cattle that roamed the stockyards back in the day not only drove the local economy, but also shaped Fort Worth and Texas culture. In the years after the Civil War, Texas became a cattle superhighway. Cowboys would round up cattle in southern Texas and drive them north on the Chisholm Trail up into Kansas. Along the way, they'd stop in Fort Worth to gather supplies. The Fort Worth Stockyards were created in 1893 to leverage this traffic—combining multiple cattle management facilities such as meatpacking plants with the town's railroad infrastructure. The company was actually incorporated in Virginia, to take advantage of that state's favorable tax laws. But the operation itself was 100 percent Texas. The stockyards became the heart and soul of Fort Worth. Although this picture was taken sometime before 1944, the exact date is unknown. But the legacy that cattle like these passed on to Forth Worth couldn't be clearer, as the city's moniker is "Cowtown."

c.1940

ABOVE: This old brick road still sees the boots of a lot of cowhands. But these days you're more likely to encounter herds of businesspeople or university students than actual livestock on the move. The Fort Worth Stockyards is now known almost exclusively as an entertainment venue— with a host of restaurants, nightclubs, hotels, and other businesses capitalizing on its cowboy heritage. Though the old cattle stockyards operated under a number of names over the years, the Fort Worth Stockyards continued to be an economic engine. In 1944 the enterprise had total receipts of more than 5.25 million animals—the largest in the history of any such market. During its peak years in the 1940s, nearly fifty companies operated within the stockyards. But the cattle industry, like all industries, changed. More decentralization in cattle marketing, logistical advancements, competition, and the urbanization of Texas eventually wound down the business.

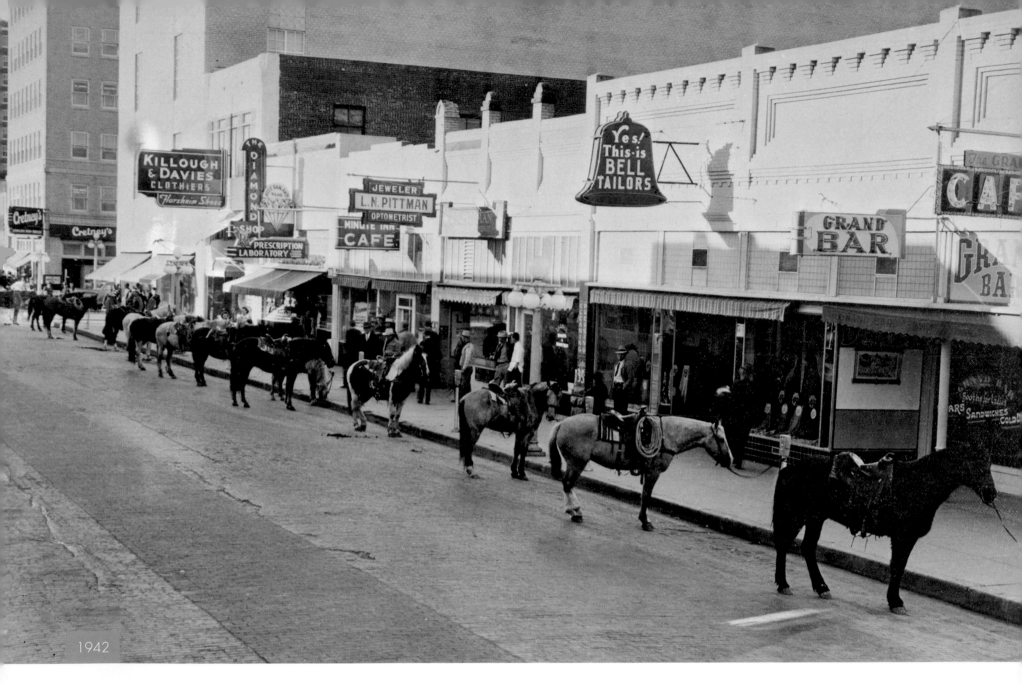

1942

PARKING METERS, AMARILLO

Horses have always been an important part of the city's culture

ABOVE: This photo was taken in 1942, just as the United States was stepping into World War II. It wasn't just the boys on the front line who did their part. In 1942 the U.S. government began rationing commodities such as metal, sugar, coffee, and rubber. Citizens limited their consumption of such items. These handsome horses are tied to the parking meters on a downtown Amarillo street. Their owners were a group of forty businessmen who took up riding their horses into town in order to conserve wear and tear on their automobiles—and to save gasoline. They felt good about doing their part for the war effort in a way that was true to their Texas ranching heritage. They felt less good about the tickets several of them received for failing to feed the meters the required nickel.

ABOVE: The City of Amarillo removed all of its parking meters in 1967, and many of those original storefronts are gone. Taking one's horse to work isn't an option for most workers in Amarillo, but it's still an option for some. And horses are still held dear here. Amarillo is home to the American Quarter Horse Hall of Fame and Museum—a tribute to the great horses and humans of the West. It's also the homestead of Charles Goodnight, who was a celebrated rancher,

Texas Ranger, and inventor of the chuck wagon in the days when cowboys still roamed the range en masse. A number of famous ranches are still in operation in the Amarillo area. The citywide art display "Hoof Prints of the American Quarter Horse" pays homage to Amarillo's equine heritage with over a hundred original fiberglass horse statues created by local artists.

1974

CADILLAC RANCH, AMARILLO
A work of art that the public can't leave alone

ABOVE: *Cadillac Ranch* was a public art installation created in 1974 by the group Ant Farm—Doug Michels, Chip Lord, and Hudson Marquez. Founded in San Francisco in 1968, Ant Farm was an avant-garde design, architectural, and environmental group known for high-profile counterculture pieces. *Cadillac Ranch* was composed of ten Cadillac automobiles, ranging in model years from 1949 to 1963, buried nose-first. What was the point? It was meant as a tribute to the rise and fall of the iconic tailfin of the time, but as with any

work of art, different people came away with various interpretations about American popular culture, materialism, art, and commerce. The project was bankrolled by Texas millionaire Stanley Marsh III. The cars were buried in a straight line facing west, starting with the 1949 Club Sedan and ending with the 1963 Sedan de Ville. *Cadillac Ranch* was installed just off of the old Route 66 west of Amarillo—a considerable distance from the town in 1974.

1974

ABOVE: This is why we can't have anything nice. Part of *Cadillac Ranch*'s charm is that graffiti is openly encouraged. Tourists from all over the world are there at all times of the day spray-painting the cars and just hanging out. On special occasions the cars all get a coat of paint—such as all pink one year in honor of Stanley Marsh's wife's birthday, or multicolored to celebrate gay pride. When Ant Farm member Doug Michels died, the cars were all painted black.

In 2002 Hampton Inn made a big public-relations push to restore national landmarks, giving the cars a fresh coat of their original colors. It lasted less than twenty-four hours. In 1997 the installation was moved from its original spot two miles directly west on the highway (now commonly known as Interstate 40).

EL PASO STREET, EL PASO
No longer a frontier town of drinking, gambling, and six-shooters

BELOW: This 1903 photograph shows the 100 block of South El Paso Street. The building on the left, built around 1883, housed Kline's Mexican and Indian Curio Company. Gunfighter John Wesley Hardin had a law office in that building (Hardin studied law while in prison). Across the street to the far right was the Grand Central Hotel. The original Grand Central Hotel, where the Mills Building stands today, burned in 1892. This building housed the *El Paso Herald* newspaper at one time, a basement eatery called the Vienna Café, a cigar shop, a number of retail stores, as well as real estate, law, and insurance offices. The building to the left of that was the Mundy Brothers Market Building, home to a large livestock-trading concern. The building offered a free reading room with "the choicest collection of papers and books on livestock and grazing interests of both the U.S. and Mexico."

RIGHT: This intermediate photo from the 1970s shows the yet-to-be-expanded Camino Real Hotel to the left of what remains of the old Victorian terrace.

c.1975

BELOW: Over the years, the street has changed but remains a vital part of the city. Hardin's office is gone (he was shot by an off-duty police officer at the Acme Saloon while he was playing dice). The Herald and Mundy Brothers Buildings were eventually replaced by the Hotel Paso Del Norte, which opened in 1912. Designed by Trost and Trost, the building cost $1.5 million to build. The man who financed it, Zack T. White, didn't want the hotel to suffer the same fate as the old original Grand Central Hotel. White sent the architect to San Francisco to study buildings that survived the 1906 earthquake, and spared no expense. During the Mexican Revolution, watching battles between the Mexican army and revolutionaries from the hotel's terrace was a popular pastime. The hotel underwent a number of renovations and expansions over the years, and in 1993 was purchased by a Mexican corporation and renamed the Camino Real Hotel.

1907

MEXICAN ADOBE HOUSE, EL PASO
The traditional building style of Texas and New Mexico

ABOVE: This classically constructed Mexican-style adobe house makes a striking scene against a backdrop of desert scrub. The photo was taken in 1907, but the general method this industrious local man used to build his house had not changed much from the original methods used by the Mesoamericans who lived here thousands of years ago. *Adobe* means "sun-dried brick." This house was basically made using an aggregate of clay, silt, sand, water, and various types of organic matter. Homes like this were built without any real insulation because of adobe's thermal properties (and El Paso's mild winters). The posts that can be seen sticking out of the walls near the roofline are used as load-bearing support for the ceiling. El Paso receives some snow, but not a huge amount. Early residents were able to build a simple flat roof without having to worry about the weight of heavy snow accumulation. Mount Franklin is visible in the background.

134

ABOVE: Adobe houses are still seen all around town. It's possible to spend $1 million on an adobe-adorned mansion, and the Southwestern adobe style of architecture can also be found in commercial and industrial buildings around the Southwest. Visitors to El Paso can tour the historic Magoffin Home—a nineteen-room adobe mansion that served as the home of El Paso pioneer Joseph Magoffin. But these traditional Southwestern houses don't have to be so grandiose; spartan simplicity is part of their appeal. Their self-reliant charm explains why they've endured for millennia not just in the southwestern United States but also in South America, the Middle East, Africa, eastern Europe, and Spain. The towers that sit atop Mount Franklin are FAA communications towers.

1902

FEDERAL BUILDING / PLAZA HOTEL, EL PASO
The Hilton towered over the city from 1936 to 1963, when it was renamed the Plaza

LEFT: This shot of El Paso's Federal Building (on the left) and the Sheldon Hotel was taken in 1902. The Federal Building was designed by architect James H. Windrim, and was completed in 1892. The facility served as a customhouse, a post office, and a courthouse. It also housed the U.S. District Court for the Western District of Texas until 1936. The Sheldon Hotel across the street was originally an office building. Dr. Lucius Sheldon, a Brooklyn native, brought an architect from his hometown to convert the building to a hotel in 1899—and spared no expense. It opened for business the next year. The hotel's dining room was the talk of the town. Interestingly, many participants of the 1910 Mexican Revolution held strategy conferences and struck gentlemen's agreements impacting the region's geopolitics over brandy and cigars at the Sheldon. Some who found themselves on the losing side wound up across the street in the courthouse.

ABOVE: The old Federal Building was razed in 1936. San Jacinto Plaza now stands in its place. A fire destroyed the Sheldon Hotel in 1929. Conrad Hilton built the seventeen-story hotel that now occupies the site. It was designed by local architects Trost and Trost, who built numerous structures in El Paso. It cost $1 million. Nineteen days after construction began, the stock market crashed and the Great Depression began. The project made it, though. The name was changed from the Hilton to the Plaza in 1963. Elizabeth Taylor lived in the hotel's penthouse for a brief time. It got a big makeover in 2008 along with the Anson Mills Building (the large building on the right). Three historical markers stand at the Plaza Hotel today—marking it as the site of the state's first kindergarten, the original location of the Women's Club of El Paso, and a critical meeting spot for the early League of United Latin American Citizens.

137

c.1975

516 SOUTH EL PASO STREET

A street once frequented by Pancho Villa, Billy the Kid, and Wyatt Earp

ABOVE: This photo from the early 1970s shows 516 South El Paso Street occupied by a secondhand clothing store (*ropa usada* means "used clothes"). Just down the street, the southern end of the street connects to Mexico via the Santa Fe Bridge. For more than 150 years, the people of both El Paso and nearby Juárez, Mexico, have prowled South El Paso Street looking for a bargain or a little fun. The street has a retail history dating to 1859, which predates the incorporation of the city in 1873. The street was once lined

with adobe buildings, but today South El Paso Street boasts the mix of architectural styles that can only come with a divergence of different cultures over time. Down the street, one can see the Art Moderne–style Teatro Colón at 509 South El Paso Street. The theater was built in 1912, catering to affluent Mexican refugees. It was one of many theaters in the area (including the nearby Teatro Alcázar, which was once used to store guns for Mexican Huertista revolutionaries).

ABOVE: Over the years, Pancho Villa, Billy the Kid, and Wyatt Earp have all walked South El Paso Street. Shoppers can still go to 516 South El Paso Street and find a bargain on clothes—and sell a little gold and silver while they're at it. The sign reading "Mayoreo Menudeo" loosely translates as "get more for less" (a similar sign appears on the old store). Many people along South El Paso Street extend their storefronts to the open air on the sidewalks. The buildings of South El Paso Street have distinctive designs, the result of a sort of retail Darwinism across 150 years of Pan American trade. The old Teatro Colón down the road is now a toy store—but the distinctive storefront is still visible. The tall building at the end of the road is the Camino Real Hotel.

c.1900

EL PASO COURTHOUSE

One of the many courthouses that have graced El Paso over the years

LEFT: El Paso County has had seven courthouses in its history. The first big one was dedicated in 1886. The elaborate, eclectic Renaissance-style building had three stories and featured a clock tower, elaborate dormers, and a grand entrance. It was topped with two alabaster statues of a woman holding a pair of balancing scales. By the turn of the century, El Paso had outgrown the building. The charming structure was razed to make room for the new 1917 courthouse designed by Trost and Trost. It included not just a courthouse but also an auditorium, jail, and farmers' market (a somehow unsettling combination). In 1955 the building's facade was completely remodeled. Where it once had a dozen grand, massive columns, the remodel gave the building a flatter and more modern look that wasn't very popular.

ABOVE: The 1917 courthouse, since occupied by city hall, was demolished in the early 1990s to make way for a new building that stands on the site. The granite front entryway, shaped like the Alamo, is about the spot where the 1917 courthouse once stood. In 1979 the city government grew out of the building and relocated west of downtown. While it's sad to consider the fate of the old 1886 and 1917 buildings, some mementos remain. The new courthouse has a twelfth-story law library, where one can find pieces of the old 1917 courthouse on display. And the two alabaster statues from the old 1886 courthouse survived the wrecking ball after all. One stands at the entrance of Ascarate Park right by the border with Mexico. The second one disappeared for a time, but was found in 1936 and placed on the lawn of the courthouse.

c.1975

HOTEL McCOY / ANSON MILLS BUILDING, EL PASO:
Part of the South El Paso Street Historic District

ABOVE: The Anson Mills Building at 303 North Oregon. The windows were remodeled in 1974 and the building was listed on the National Register of Historic Places in 2011.

LEFT: The two large buildings in the middle are the Hotel McCoy (left), which also housed the popular White House Department Store, and the Anson Mills Building (right). The Hotel McCoy was designed by Henry C. Trost, and sports a style reminiscent of famed Chicago architect Louis Henry Sullivan. The Anson Mills Building next door was also designed by Trost. Completed in 1911, it was America's second concrete-frame skyscraper (the Ingalls Building in Cincinnati was the first). The Anson Mills Building is an historic building located at 303 North Oregon Street in El Paso. The building stands on the original site of the 1832 Ponce de León ranch.

ABOVE: The White House Department Store eventually linked with the Anson Mills Building in the 1920s as part of a $1 million deal. At the time, the store sported the longest single-span escalator in the country. The store changed hands a few times before closing its doors in 1983. The Mills Building has had a number of upgrades over the years. In 1974 it swapped out its windows for mirrored glass, and it recently underwent a major overhaul that was completed in 2010. Both buildings are now listed on the National Register of Historic Places.

LEFT: The Pioneer Plaza movie theater at 125 South El Paso Street before it got a Spanish Mission style makeover (visible in the modern image above).